C0-ATN-621

BOOKS ABOUT HAWAII

Books about Hawaii

FIFTY BASIC AUTHORS

A. GROVE DAY

THE UNIVERSITY PRESS OF HAWAII
HONOLULU

Manufactured in the United States of America

Library of Congress Cataloging in Publication Data

Day, Arthur Grove, 1904-
Books about Hawaii.

Includes index.
1. Hawaii—Book reviews. 2. Bibliography—Best books—Hawaii. 3. Hawaii—Bibliography.
I. Title.
DU620.5.D39 016.9969 77-7997
ISBN 0-8248-0561-5

Dedicated to
my fellow residents of Arcadia,
who have time to enjoy reading Hawaiiana

Contents

Preface

GOOD READING ABOUT THE FIFTIETH STATE

"What should I read about Hawaii?"
More than twenty thousand bound volumes are to be found in the Hawaiian Collection of the University of Hawaii Library. Many people are amazed to learn that such a deluge of words has been printed concerning a North Pacific archipelago. To answer this question, I have spent more than thirty years browsing in that outstanding collection, seeking volumes that have literary merit—that, in other words, would be enjoyed by any reader regardless of the island setting.

For historical reasons, Hawaii has a literary heritage more varied than that of most other American states. It derives from a group of subtropical islands far from any continent, settled more than a millennium ago by Polynesian canoe-voyagers bringing with them a skilled culture developed under severe South Sea conditions. After centuries of civil conflict, one outstanding ruler emerged, unifying the islands through the aid of European wanderers who had come there after the men of Captain James Cook's expedition had revealed the existence of the archipelago to the outside world. The Kamehameha dynasty, often, after 1819, with the advice of American missionaries, was replaced in 1872 by elected monarchs. Geographical, economic, and educational influences led increasingly to an American hegemony over the islands, and several years after a revolution led by pro-annexation residents, the American flag first flew over the group in 1898. The assimilation of immigrants from half a dozen Asian and Pacific countries finally resulted in a modern community that is a showcase of American democracy in

Oceania. Hawaii became the fiftieth state of the Union in 1959.

The literature of Hawaii embodies the best writings about this fascinating region, the books that evoke the flavor and allure of the "Paradise of the Pacific." Until now, although several million visitors come annually to view the varied wonders of the islands, the need for an introduction to this branch of literature in English has not been met. With twenty thousand books to choose from, discernment is certainly required. A selective, annotated guide through this mass of printed material is herein supplied, in the hope of aiding the visitor, the student, the teacher, the collector, the librarian, and—most of all—the informed reader who enjoys losing himself in tales of demigods and ghosts, voyagers by canoe or frigate, castaways, beachcombers, seekers of the "noble savage," escapists from over-civilized areas, missionaries, sandalwood traders, deserters and convicts, whalemen, brown-skinned Polynesian monarchs, scientists and travelers, sun-seeking artists and poets, yachtsmen, and visiting authors of world renown.

What types of literature are prominent? The customary history of American writing, for example, begins with oral records of the aboriginal beliefs and customs, logs of sea explorers, regional histories, memoirs, journals and diaries, missionary reports, travels, and even sermons. These are the types that one generally finds in any study of a frontier region. The works may, also, have modest claims to literary merit and charm, are often fresh and interesting, and give valuable insights into the places, times, and events involved; further, they may provide background and other material for later, more creative writers. It is not surprising that the types of authorship found early in the history of Hawaii, another frontier region, should follow this pattern.

The native literature of Hawaii, like that of the rest of the Polynesian Triangle, was not written, but was handed down by word of mouth—often through many generations of trained bards and reciters of genealogies. Oratory was a great Polynesian art, and the speaker stirred his listeners with sparkling metaphors and allusions to classic stories. The court of a nobleman always included a poet whose duty it was to compose chants and to recite genealogies. There was also a class of strolling minstrels who entertained the villagers with folk tales and stories of heroes. A sport of the nobility, in which lives were often at stake, was the literary tournament; the contestants rivaled each other in composing songs and in riddling, punning, reciting the names of persons and places, and competing in other tests of wit and word play. The hula was not only a dance but a religious art that took the place of our concert hall and lecture room, our opera and theater. Hence the collected lore of Hawaii provides a fertile source of knowledge about the history, traditions, customs, arts, and religious ideals of these early people. The tone of the literature is primarily aristocratic, however, and the common folk merely serve to set off the exploits of their gods, heroes, and chiefs.

Hawaiian literary style is marked by exaggeration, humor, antithesis, and the use of revealing details in characterization. Names of persons and regions are repeated again and again: such catalogs were recited with great enjoyment. (Later, when the missionaries came, they found that their pupils liked best to memorize those parts of the Bible that list the "begats.") Both prose and poetry are filled with simile and symbolism, drawn mainly from the various aspects of nature—rain, flowers, forests, the moon.

The first written records of native literature come from James Cook and his crew members—including several Polynesians from Tahiti, who found the Hawaiian language quite similar to their own. No standard scheme of writing Hawaiian speech in a roman alphabet was used until the early 1820s, when a group of Protestant missionaries limited the letters to seventeen, which in 1826 were further reduced to twelve. The five vowels were given the Italian pronunciation; these, together with seven consonants—*h, k, l, m, n, p,* and *w*—enabled any Hawaiian word to be written. It was then possible not only to begin translating the Bible and other worthy works into Hawaiian but to permit the Hawaiian people to write down their stories and recollections in their own language, to be translated later by others. Wide shelves of books in Hawaiian may be found in the libraries of the islands, and language courses are given that enable students today to enjoy this body of aboriginal writing.

My selection of books to review begins, then, with works by persons of Hawaiian blood, in English translation. Translators of such caliber as Martha Beckwith, Nathaniel B. Emerson, William Hyde Rice, Mary Kawena Pukui, Katharine Luomala, Samuel H. Elbert, and Alfons L. Korn have given us volumes that re-create the wealth of myth, legend, and song transmitted through the ages on Polynesian islands. Native authors such as David Malo, Samuel M. Kamakau, S. N. Haleole, Kepelino Keauokalani, and John Ii are well represented in translation, partly as a result of the movement that started among the teachers of history at the mission high school at Lahainaluna, Maui, in the latter 1830s.

The writing of the history of the Hawaiian Islands, in fact, began before the modern reader might imagine that there was very much history to record. The Reverend Sheldon Dibble published at Lahainaluna in 1843 his *History of the Sandwich Islands,* incorporating much of the material gathered orally by his students among their village elders. The first solid history by a professional author (who was also the first to publish a novel based on the lore of the islands) was written by James J. Jarves, and also appeared in 1843, along with a companion volume of travel essays. A history of Hawaii by one who had never visited the islands was written in London by Manley Hopkins and appeared in 1862. The practice of documentary history culminated in 1967 with *The Hawaiian Kingdom,* the monumental three-volume work by Ralph S. Kuykendall. Kuykendall also wrote a one-volume history of the islands, as have contemporary writers Gavan Daws, A. Grove Day, Gerrit P. Judd, W. Storrs Lee, and Edward Joesting. Day (in collaboration with Carl Stroven), Judd, and Lee have also compiled anthologies of writings in English about Hawaii.

The historical dividing line in Hawaiian history is, of course, the discovery of the group in 1778 by Captain James Cook, R.N., during his third Pacific voyage. Castaways from European or Asian vessels may have reached Hawaiian shores in previous times, but until Cook's two ships sighted the northwestern three islands, no knowledge of the interesting culture of these Polynesian settlers in the North Pacific had reached beyond the region. The journals of Cook and his men—who were often skillful in describing what they saw—is the source at which students of Hawaiian civilization must start; for changes began to affect that fragile life-style even on the two nights when twenty seamen were stormbound on the islet of Niihau in January 1778. The accounts by Cook, James King, David Samwell, and others of the voyagers are the primary sources for studies of "ancient" Hawaiian customs, beliefs, and language; changes were reported even as soon as Nathaniel Portlock, George Dixon, and George Vancouver (all of whom had been in Cook's crews) led trading voyages to Hawaii a few years later.

Accounts by such traders—along with those of sea wanderers like the indomitable Archibald Campbell, the semi-pirate Peter Corney, and Captain Amasa Delano—supplement the reading of more formal historians. Among the explorers from other nations who hoped to vie with Cook in Pacific empire-building, Otto von Kotzebue, son of a celebrated German dramatist, is the most engrossing storyteller. Kotzebue was an officer on three visits by Russian ships. The Russian filibustering efforts around 1815, which planted the Czar's flag over the island of Kauai, inspired a historical novel by Darwin Teilhet.

The Protestant mission program centered in Boston, aiming at Christianizing the Hawaiian Islands, has produced a voluminous quantity of writing, which indeed fills the shelves of the Hawaiian Mission Children's Library, located in downtown Honolulu. Much of this material is quite readable, in spite of its pious intent. The little memoir of the Hawaiian lad called Henry Obookiah, who inspired the launching of the first shipload of missionaries that landed in the "Sandwich Islands" in 1820, is only the first of many volumes about this high-minded effort.

Foremost among the ministers of the Gospel who arrived in the *Thaddeus* in that critical year was the Reverend Hiram Bingham. His book about the twenty-one years he and his family spent in Hawaii is not limited to mission doings, but encompasses general observation of Hawaiian life during these and other years; it is history in which the historian had a quite active part.

Another member of the "First Company" of missionaries was Lucy Goodale Thurston, who spent the rest of her life in the islands and whose memoirs revive the excitements of that pioneer time. Another was Elisha Loomis, first printer in the North Pacific region, who with his wife labored seven years in God's vineyard—their story is told in Albertine Loomis's *Grapes of Canaan,* the best documentary novel of the early period. Another was Dr. Thomas Holman, Hawaii's first physician, who fills the opening chapters of Francis Halford's *9 Doctors and God,* the story of the medical missionaries and other practitioners in the islands up to the twentieth century.

The most lively general account of the mission era is that by Bradford Smith, author of *Yankees in Paradise: The New England Impact on Hawaii.* He tells of the men and women who labored between 1820 and 1854, and of the problems they had to face. Prominent among the early workers were William Ellis, an energetic Englishman with experience in the South Pacific, and Charles S. Stewart, who helped to set up the first mission at Lahaina. Stewart's colleagues had bad as well as good experiences, such as suffering attacks by enraged seamen like "Mad Jack" Percival, commander of the *Dolphin,* first American warship to visit Honolulu, who resented restrictions upon visits aboard by complaisant Hawaiian maidens. The *Dolphin* story is told by First Lieutenant Hiram Paulding.

A medical missionary whose executive ability finally led him to leave the mission and embark upon the choppy waters of politics in the progressive kingdom was Dr. Gerrit P. Judd. He is the leading figure in Samuel Harrison's novel *The White King,* a historical narrative that departs only slightly from fact. This story is supplemented by the diary of his wife, Laura Fish Judd, who faithfully supported his moves and also bore him nine children—some of whose descendants, like those of the Thurstons, are still living in Hawaii today.

The life of the islands in 1840 is graphically presented by the American traveler and artist Frederick A. Olmsted in *Incidents of a Whaling Voyage.* In the following year, the United States Exploring Expedition, the most ambitious scientific fleet hitherto sent out by any nation, arrived in Hawaii and began ransacking the islands for data of many sorts. Under the command of Charles Wilkes, a large party ascended snowcapped Mauna Loa and the workers spent three weeks in tents on the windy summit, making measurements at an elevation of almost fourteen thousand feet. The chapters on Hawaii in the voluminous report of the expedition made the world realize, almost for the first time, the wonders of the North Pacific archipelago that was not too far away from the western shore of the American continent.

Herman Melville, whose ramblings in the South Seas were to result in such novels as *Typee, Omoo,* and *Moby Dick,* was discharged from a whale ship at Lahaina in May 1843, and soon went to Honolulu, where, after serving as a pinsetter in a bowling alley, he signed an indenture as a clerk in a British general store. This attachment explains his defense, in an appendix to *Typee,* of the illegal annexation of the Hawaiian Islands in that year by Lord George Paulet, commander of the British frigate *Carysfort.* Melville was shocked by the saturnalia that followed the restoration of Hawaiian sovereignty by Admiral Richard Thomas on July 31. This short piece is the only factual writing by Melville about Hawaii, for he enlisted in an American vessel after only ten weeks; but elsewhere in *Typee* and in other books, such as *Mardi,* he does refer to his Hawaiian sojourn.

The "manifest destiny" of the United States to expand into the world's largest ocean brought travelers who, like George Washington Bates in 1853, toured the islands and recommended that a pending treaty between Kamehameha III and the United States should result in annexation of the kingdom.

The possibility that filibusters from California might achieve such an outcome by violence fills the opening chapter of *Ka'a'awa: A Novel About Hawaii in the 1850s,* by O. A. Bushnell. Dr. Bushnell, a professor of microbiology, is the foremost novelist born in Hawaii, and *Ka'a'awa*—the name of a village and valley on the North Shore of Oahu—is the third in his series of fine historical novels, beginning with one on the last days of Captain Cook.

The rise of the sugar industry in the islands, which replaced whaling as an economic mainstay, is told in the history of three prominent families, in *Koamalu* by Ethel M. Damon, an author who wrote other volumes dealing mainly with the later wave of missionaries and their descendants.

Richard Henry Dana, Jr. (1815–1882), Boston lawyer and author of *Two Years Before the Mast,* arrived in Honolulu in the autumn of 1859 on a British sailing ship that had rescued him and some two hundred others from a burning passenger vessel. He was made welcome by many residents of the city, including King Kamehameha IV and the court circle. After adventures on Oahu, Maui, and the Big Island, he was unable to find a ship that would permit him to continue his trip around the world, and he boarded a vessel that returned him to San Francisco. Aside from a chapter in the third volume of his *Journal,* however, Dana wrote little about Hawaii (see Appendix A).

During the middle of the past century began the fashion of considering the Hawaiian Islands a target for tourism—an industry that today brings in more income than the growing of sugar cane and pineapple put together. Among the first of these were Lady Jane Franklin, widow of the Arctic explorer, and her companion Sophia Cracroft, who left their impressions of the kingdom on the eve of the American Civil War, as told in *The Victorian Visitors* by Alfons L. Korn.

Just after that war, Samuel L. Clemens, a journalist who was beginning to use the pseudonym "Mark Twain," spent four months journeying around the islands and writing a series of travel letters for a California newspaper. Flavored with his typical wry humor, these accounts contain much serious observation on life in the kingdom, and were the basis for the speech that embarked Clemens on a highly successful career as a lecturer. The collected *Letters from Hawaii,* if published at that time, would have been Mark Twain's first book.

Other celebrated authors of travel books covered Hawaii

during the next century. Among these were two British writers, Isabella Bird Bishop, who wrote *The Hawaiian Archipelago,* and Constance F. Gordon-Cumming, author of *Fire Fountains.*

Anthony Trollope, the prolific Victorian author, made two short visits to Honolulu, in October 1872 and in September 1875. On both occasions he was returning from visiting his son in Australia, and each time spent less than twenty-four hours in the city. About half of the nineteenth letter in his collection, *The Tireless Traveler* (Berkeley: University of California Press, 1941, ed. Bradford A. Booth), written after the second stop, is concerned with facts about the kingdom, but all could have been gleaned from two available guide books and from the history by Jarves.

Many admirers of Edward Bellamy, author of the utopian novel *Looking Backward,* are not aware that as a young man he made a visit to Hawaii. Seeking health, Edward and his ailing brother Frederick arrived from San Francisco around the first of March 1878. After his return to New England, Edward published in the magazine *Good Company* (5, 1880, pp. 8–15) a "frame story" called "A Tale of the South Pacific." Told by a native of "one of the remoter islands" to a party overtaken by night at the edge of the glowing Kilauea Volcano, the tale recounts the adventure of a white castaway who, by the use of ventriloquism, escapes his fate among South Sea cannibals. The author describes himself as "a mere tourist person, drawn to these remote regions by a desire dating from the perusal of *Robinson Crusoe* to behold a genuine Polynesian island, ere yet its primitive people should have succumbed in the effort to grapple with the philosophy of clothes and all that it implies."

A dreamy lotus-eater and romantic writer of sketches was Charles Warren Stoddard, who produced several collections of essays dealing with Hawaii and the South Seas. It was Stoddard who, in San Francisco, inspired tubercular Robert Louis Stevenson to spend his last years in the tropical zone of the Pacific.

Stevenson is one of the best-known authors to have spent some time in Hawaii, and his observations on the islands, in prose and verse, have been collected in a volume supplementing such fiction as "The Bottle Imp," "The Isle of Voices," and *The Wrecker*. His celebrated "Open Letter to the Reverend Dr. Hyde of Honolulu," a searing attack on a Protestant clergyman who made the mistake of slandering Father Damien, "martyr of Molokai," still offers fuel for spirited debate in Hawaii.

Political satire arose as a timely literary form around the middle 1880s, when the corruption of the reign of King Kalakaua became a target of scorn. A pamphlet appeared in 1886 entitled *The Grand Duke of Gynbergdrinkenstein: a Burlesque in Three Acts* (Honolulu: privately printed), which was "respectfully dedicated to the Public of the Duchy, Honolulu, H.I., 1886." In the rather heavy-handed ridicule, "Herr von Boss" is Claus Spreckels and "Nosbig" is Walter Murray Gibson, an adviser to the king in several scandalous adventures. The play is attributed to Alatau T. Atkinson, editor of the Hawaiian *Gazette* and later minister of public instruction, in collaboration with Edward William Purvis. These two satirists presumably also worked together on some sprightly verse, *The Gynberg Ballads* (Honolulu: privately printed, n.d.), an illustrated pamphlet, printed in color. Purvis's brother claimed that Edward wrote all the ballads and did the illustrations. The humor barely conceals a warm indignation at the attempt by the court to sell the rights to import opium into the kingdom, and to presume to attain "primacy of the Pacific" through outfitting a guano-hauling windjammer as a Hawaiian gunboat to overawe island groups to the southward. Among those figuring in the *Ballads* are Gibson (then foreign minister), Sam Parker, Attorney General Antone Rosa, Curtis Iaukea, "Marshal" Kaulukou, Captain George E. G. Jackson of the *Kaimiloa,* and Gibson's son-in-law, F. H. Hayselden.

At this same time appeared *Vacuum, a Farce in Three Acts* (Honolulu: privately printed, n.d.), in conventional playlet form, by an author who was later to head the government for an entire decade. This was Sanford Ballard Dole, future president of the republic of Hawaii and first territorial governor. Kalakaua is satirized under the title of "Skyhigh Emperor of the Coral Reefs and Sand Banks of the Big Blue Sea." His cabinet includes the "Extravaganzies and Incompetents" like Palaver (Gibson), Cockade, Calabash, and Picnic; Bananagan, Lord High Pipelighter to His Most Imperial Majesty; and Mango, First Kahili Bearer. It is likely that such propaganda had an effect upon the success of the Hawaiian League and the signing by Kalakaua of the concessive "Bayonet Constitution" of 1887.

The downfall of the monarchy and the rule by a provisional government, led by pro-annexation citizens, has been told by its leading figure, Lydia Liliuokalani, in *Hawaii's Story by Hawaii's Queen,* published in the year when the islands first lay under the Stars and Stripes. Both the revolution of 1893 and the ceremony of annexation in 1898 brought world attention to Hawaii, and a number of writers came to the islands in journalistic mood.

"Joaquin Miller," Western poet and poseur, visited Hawaii in the spring of 1895, the period of the counter-revolution that failed to overthrow the republic. On duty as reporter, attired in leather leggings and a wide sombrero, he was found wandering around "the front" in Manoa Valley by a government officer. Miller had the effrontery to call upon President Dole, accompanied by his pregnant mistress, whom he introduced as the wife of his California plumber. Mrs. Dole discovered the deception and suggested that the pair leave the islands. Miller later published an article, "Kamehameha the Great" (*Overland Monthly,* series 2, 25, June 1895), which contains general remarks on Hawaiian life and people. He makes an interesting comment concerning Robert Louis Stevenson: "I am told that he often took steerage, although a very sick man; he wanted to see, to hear, and so he kept where he could learn something in the mighty university of humanity."

Other visitors who wrote about the islands during the revolutionary decade include Charles G. Nottage, Dr. Edward S. Goodhue, and Mary H. Krout.

The twentieth century ushered in an era of territorial rule. "They don't know what they've got!" exclaimed Jack London about the American people when he landed in the Territory of Hawaii in 1907, on the first leg of a yachting cruise through the Pacific with his new wife Charmian. The California storyteller explored many corners of this offshore territory of the United States during a five-month stay, and the couple returned to Hawaii as their second home in 1915 and 1916. Two volumes of short stories and several other pieces by Jack have been collected as *Stories of Hawaii.* In her own right, Charmian is to be considered in the list, as author of such volumes as *The Log of the "Snark"* and *Our Hawaii.*

Among many other twentieth-century writers about Hawaii may be named Armine von Tempski, who was encouraged by Jack London to write such books as her popular autobiography *Born in Paradise.* Earl Derr Biggers, the creator of the celestial detective Charlie Chan, wrote *The House Without a Key* as a result of a visit to Honolulu. University teachers like Ruth Eleanor McKee, O. A. Bushnell, and Marjorie Sinclair have enriched the growing shelf of solid fiction with Hawaiian settings. The impact of the "blitz" on Pearl Harbor in 1941 elicited not only factual books like Blake Clarke's *Remember Pearl Harbor!* and Walter Lord's *Day of Infamy* but wartime fiction like James Jones' *From Here to Eternity* and *The Pistol.* Since those years of conflict, the most notable novel about the islands—a giant panorama covering the millions of years from the emergence of the archipelago from the depths of the ocean to an imaginary election campaign in 1954—is James A. Michener's pageant of Pacific assimilation, simply titled *Hawaii.*

Aside from translations of native chants and songs, few outstanding examples of poetry in English have come from Hawaii. The inhabitants have been less occupied in voicing high dreams in verse than in assimilating newcomers from other lands and in building a sturdy economy. Then, too, the lushness of the surroundings may lead to a similar unpruned luxuriance in outpourings inspired by swaying palm fronds and hula skirts.

Visiting poets have voiced their feelings about Hawaii. Both Stevenson and Stoddard produced verses with island settings. Rupert Brooke, the young English poet, during a short stay in 1913 wrote one of his finest sonnets, "Waikiki." World War II brought to the islands, staging area for the Pacific conflict, a million men that included several young poets, among them William Meredith, Louis O. Coxe, and Donald Stauffer. The best poet to grow up in Hawaii is undoubtedly Genevieve Taggard, but she departed at the age of twenty and wrote little verse about the tropics. More recent names come to mind—Don Blanding, Lloyd Stone, and Clifford Gessler. At present, a number of competent poets center around the University of Hawaii—among them Phyllis Thompson, John Logan, and John Unterecker. Not all of these, however, have chosen the Hawaiian setting for their verse. One may hope that their example may inspire some of the polyracial young people of the community to produce, in the not too distant future, the fine poetry that Hawaii deserves.

The drama is an even more difficult genre to create in a community that has still not agreed upon its fundamental standards. Many plays are produced in the islands, but few by local playwrights. Jean Charlot—an artist who writes in both English and Hawaiian—Aldyth Morris, and John Kneubuhl, among others, have had plays produced. The lively department of drama at the University of Hawaii may be expected to elicit playable scripts, in English or in other languages.

The literature of Hawaii, when compared with that of larger regions, may not be outstanding. Yet few authors anywhere are Shakespeares or Miltons. If the authors of Hawaiian writings are to be classed as "minor," one should remember the remarks of Newton Arvin in his book *Longfellow:* "Americans are notoriously obsessed with the question of status, and to say that a writer is a minor writer, to many American readers, is as if one were to say that he is negligible. This is not true, or it is much less true, in Europe, where steadily, through the most seismic upheavals of taste, writers of the second or even the third order continue to be edited, to be published, and to be read. They are often, too, the objects of thoughtful critical discussion, and the general consciousness is appreciably enriched as a result. By an understandable paradox, we are much more 'democratic' in our receptiveness, and much less catholic. Our memories, too, are shorter, and once a writer has receded from the foreground of our attention, he runs the risk of being forgotten irretrievably, especially if he can be disposed of as a minor writer.'' Good books about Hawaii are not so prevalent that we can afford to discard any of them.

This book is a companion to my previous volume, *Pacific Islands Literature: One Hundred Basic Books* (Honolulu: University Press of Hawaii, 1971), and follows the same general scheme of presenting good reading material from a Pacific area. I have selected fifty authors of books about Hawaii to review at more or less length, and in the appendixes have annotated three times that many. I have not attempted to set up a strict canon to limit the pleasures of individual discovery, but have merely tried to demonstrate the rich variety of literary offerings in English from the fiftieth state. It is quite possible that some of the titles in the appendixes should have been included among the fifty, and others demoted. I hope I have not overlooked anyone's favorite classic. I have not defined ''literature'' for my purpose so rigidly as to omit from consideration anything quite readable. Although all the books deal with the general setting of the Hawaiian Islands, my test is whether the book chosen would be read for its charm or power, regardless of setting.

All the books—except for a few reference works listed in Appendix C—are considered, then, to offer pleasurable perusal. Deliberately omitted are textbooks, scientific works, guide books, special volumes such as almanacs and cookbooks, and items for children. Works mentioned are in the English language. Some, of course, are translations. One more qualified than I might well write a comparable work on books about Hawaii in tongues other than English. For example, persons of Japanese ancestry in Hawaii, I am told, have written in their language several hundred books, including histories, biographies, reminiscences, essays, novels, and poems.

My purpose, then, is to share with other readers some results of my haunting of the Hawaiian Collection in the University of Hawaii Library for more than thirty years, and to make known my opinions of selected volumes that have literary value. My choices are influenced by half a lifetime of research spent on the literature that has come from the Pacific region. During this time I have edited ten volumes of anthologies of such literature, five of them in collaboration with my colleague Carl Stroven. It was he who originated, forty years ago, the course in "Literature of the Pacific" that has been given at least once each year since that time at the University of Hawaii—a unique course which I had the pleasure of offering for a decade and which is now given by several others in Honolulu. My appreciation of the aid and suggestions coming from the staff of the University Library, as well as the responses of students and other readers, is warmly acknowledged here.

Users of this book should be aware of some of the methods followed. The fifty main reviews deal with the outstanding work of each chosen author. Information is also given about other writings on Hawaii by these authors, with some pertinent biographical data. Books on similar subjects by other writers are sometimes mentioned.

The arrangement by number is chronological, based on the date of the first episode in any series of events covered. The first items are general works, or deal with prehistory and folklore; then, with the journals of James Cook, begins the period of documentary history, followed by accounts by other voyagers and adventurers, coming down to the period of statehood. Reading these reviews in this order might serve as a rough outline of the history of Hawaii as well as of the history of the literature of Hawaii.

The length of a review is not necessarily an indication of a work's importance. The title numbers are used for cross-references in the reviews; the account of William Hyde Rice, for example, naturally directs the reader to a later volume giving the history of his family. The index of authors covers all mentions of a writer, not only in this preface and in the main reviews but in the appendixes. In each entry, first editions are given. An American edition precedes others, even though a British edition might have antedated it. The names of publishers, although requiring much research, should be of value in tracing editions. Later editions, especially paperback reprints, are frequently mentioned, but no attempt has been made to indicate all transitory republication.

My choices have not been concerned with the present availability of copies. One additional value of this book, it is hoped, is that it might encourage the growing tendency to reprint—perhaps with scholarly introductions—a number of the fine works that have not yet been recognized by those publishers who have discovered the demand for new editions of what might be termed Hawaiian classics.

If you will read most or all of my fifty basic books—which would, I believe, form a good start to a bookshelf of Hawaiian literature in any library—you will qualify, certainly, as an authority when someone asks: "What should I read about Hawaii?"

[1] MARTHA BECKWITH (trans.). *The Kumulipo: A Hawaiian Creation Chant.* Chicago: University of Chicago Press, 1951; Honolulu: University Press of Hawaii, 1972.

Suggesting comparison with the Hebrew *Genesis,* the Hawaiian *Kumulipo* (the word means "origin" or "source of life") is a sacred creation chant and a genealogy of one of the great alii or ruling families, traced from the beginning of the world. An authentic primitive poem of more than two thousand lines, it was carried in memory from one generation of court reciters to another. The volume includes an English translation of the chant, as well as the original Hawaiian, with detailed commentary and social and historical background.

The opening lines give some idea of the tenor of the poem:

At the time when the earth became hot
At the time when the heavens turned about
At the time when the sun was darkened
To cause the moon to shine
The time of the rise of the Pleiades
The slime, this was the source of the earth
The source of the darkness that made darkness
The source of the night that made night
The intense darkness, the deep darkness
Darkness of the sun, darkness of the night
Nothing but night . . .

Then follow many lines cataloging the births of sea creatures and plant life. Read literally, the chant "seems to picture the rising of the land out of the fathomless depths of the ocean. Along its shores the lower forms of life begin to gather, and these are arranged as births from parent to child." Like most Hawaiian poetry, however, it has meanings hidden in symbolic language; essentially "it is a birth chant, and procreation is its theme."

Martha Beckwith (1871–1959), who spent her childhood in Hawaii and as a young woman became an acknowledged authority on Hawaiian folklore, was for many years a professor at Vassar College. Besides her edition of *The Kumulipo,* she published a number of other studies of native Hawaiian literature, including a comprehensive survey of the subject, *Hawaiian Mythology* (New Haven, Conn.: Yale University Press, 1940; Honolulu: University of Hawaii Press, 1970), with very valuable summaries of legends in various versions.

A lengthy prose romance by S. N. Haleole was translated by Beckwith under the title *The Hawaiian Romance of Laieikawai* (Washington, D.C.: 33rd Annual Report of the Bureau of American Ethnology, 1911–1912, reprinted 1918). This literal translation of what might be termed an ancient Hawaiian novel is the romance of a girl who journeys about until of marriageable age, and after several suitors fail to win her, secures a high chief for a husband, but is deserted for a younger relative.

Beckwith also translated *Traditions of Hawaii* by Kepelino Keauokalani (Honolulu: Bishop Museum, 1932; New York: Kraus, 1971). This work is controversial, since its authenticity can be questioned on the grounds of internal evidence; it was written down by the Catholic bishop L. D. Maigret, and much of it bears a striking resemblance to the Christian Bible.

[2] DAVID MALO. *Hawaiian Antiquities (Ka Moolelo Hawaii).* Translated by Nathaniel B. Emerson. Honolulu: Hawaiian Gazette Co., 1903.

All students of ancient Hawaiian culture must depend heavily upon the classic work by David Malo, translated into English under the title of *Hawaiian Antiquities.* Born in 1795 not far from the historic bay of Kealakekua, where Captain James Cook met his death, Malo during his youth was a retainer of the high chief Kuakini, brother of Queen Kaahu-

Lahainaluna Mission High School, from an engraving on copper made at the school and used in David Malo's *Hawaiian Antiquities*.

manu. Soon after the arrival of the New England missionaries he became a Christian. In 1831 he entered the mission high school at Lahainaluna on the island of Maui, set up to train young Hawaiians to become ministers. Endowed with an alert and inquiring mind, he devoted himself to the study and writing (in the Hawaiian language) of the history and customs of his people. He died in 1853 at Kalepolepo, Maui, where he had been pastor of the Congregational church.

A movement was started at Lahainaluna around 1838 by the Reverend Sheldon Dibble, who conducted a kind of seminar in which his students collected material about the Hawaiian past. A volume of this research was published by the school press in that year, under the title of *Ka Moolelo Hawaii.* A partial translation of this book, made by the Reverend Reuben Tinker, was issued serially in 1839 and 1840. In 1841 the Royal Hawaiian Historical Society was formed at Lahainaluna. Some of the further researches of the members were incorporated into Dibble's *History of the Sandwich Islands* (Lahainaluna, 1843).

Malo's volume, written around 1840, was not translated until 1903; the translation was published with an introduction by W. D. Alexander. The second edition (1951, reprinted 1971) was completely reset and slightly corrected. A revised translation is being prepared by the Bishop Museum.

"We have the testimony," says the Alexander introduction, "of one who was born and grew up to manhood under the tabu system, who had himself been a devout worshipper of the old gods, who had been brought up at the royal court, and who was considered by his countrymen as an authority on the subjects on which he afterwards wrote." Some of these subjects include pre-European daily life, geographical terms, land and water divisions, plants and animals, food and drink, household objects, classes of people, religion, healing, magic, canoes, festivals, agriculture, fishing, sports, and ancient heroes.

A fellow student of Malo at Lahainaluna was Samuel Manaiakalani Kamakau, born at Waialua, Oahu, in October 1815. Kamakau entered the school in 1833 and remained there for seven years, both as pupil and as teacher's assistant. With several others, he carried on historical research under Dibble. Kamakau married and began teaching on Maui. At one time he held the post of district judge at Wailuku, but after slightly more than a year on the bench was removed for malfeasance. From 1851 until his death in 1876, he served many times in the legislature of the kingdom. He began publishing in June 1865 the first of more than two hundred newspaper articles. From these two volumes, both translated by Mary K. Pukui (see No. 12), have issued: *The Ruling Chiefs of Hawaii* (Honolulu: Kamehameha Schools Press, 1961) and *Ka Po'e Kahiko: The People of Old* (Honolulu: Bishop Museum Press, 1964).

Another member of the Lahaina group was S. N. Haleole, author of *The Hawaiian Romance of Laieikawai,* translated by Martha Beckwith (see No. 1). He was born about 1819 and entered Lahainaluna in 1834.

A valuable book of early memoirs in the native language is *Fragments of Hawaiian History* (Honolulu: Bishop Museum Press, 1959), by John Papa Ii, who joined the court of

Kamehameha I at the age of ten and became the companion of the future Kamehameha II. The selections, translated by Mrs. Pukui and edited by Dorothy Barrère, were made from articles appearing in the newspaper *Kuokoa* from 1866 through 1870.

[3] NATHANIEL B. EMERSON. *Unwritten Literature of Hawaii: The Sacred Songs of the Hula.* Washington, D.C.: Bureau of American Ethnology, 1909; Rutland, Vt.: Tuttle, 1965.

Dr. Nathaniel B. Emerson's knowledge of the ancient customs and lore of the Hawaiians, as well as his skill in translating their songs and chants, is evident in his volume on the sacred songs of the hula. His translations are dependable, and his essays on the traditional cultivation of Polynesian dancing and reverence for ancient gods broaden the scope of his volume. His knowledge of the Hawaiian people enabled him to convey the spirit of certain native expressions or figures of speech in English phrases with similar connotations, but occasionally he marred his effect by use of stilted, outworn phrases or jarring allusions to other mythologies. Emerson's descriptions of the function of the hula in Polynesian culture, the gathering of materials from the forest and the building of the dance house, the invocations recited to placate the gods and spirits, and the organization of the hula troupe make clear that, originally, this well-known Hawaiian dance was a sophisticated religious ritual.

Born at Waialua, Oahu, of missionary parents, Emerson (1839–1915) spent some years in the United States as college student, soldier in the Civil War, medical graduate, and practicing physician. After returning to Hawaii in 1878 he served as inspector of lepers. He found time also to translate Hawaiian works such as David Malo's *Hawaiian Antiquities* (see No. 2) and the extended myth *Pele and Hiiaka* (Honolulu: Star-Bulletin, 1915), which is probably the best literary treatment in English of an authentic Hawaiian "novel."

Double-hulled Polynesian sailing craft discover the shores of Hawaii. Illustration by Joseph Feher from Katharine Luomala's *Voices on the Wind.*

[4] **KATHARINE LUOMALA.** *Voices on the Wind: Polynesian Myths and Chants.* Illus. Honolulu: Bishop Museum Press, 1955.

An entertaining literary treatment of Polynesian poetry is presented by a leading Pacific anthropologist, Katharine Luomala, an emeritus professor at the University of Hawaii.

Drawing upon many sources, Luomala retells the legends

of Maui, Tinirau, and Rata, and tales about the menehune, the helpful "little people" of island folk literature. She is the foremost authority on these dwarflike, night-working engineers, who are credited with building many temple platforms, fishponds, and watercourses on the island of Kauai.

Katharine Luomala was born in 1907 in Minnesota, and obtained three degrees at the University of California at Berkeley. She did field work among the American Indians and in the Gilbert Islands of Micronesia. For some years she was editor of the *Journal of American Folklore.* Her scholarly monographs include *Maui-of-a-Thousand-Tricks: His Oceanic and European Biographers* (Honolulu: Bishop Museum Bulletin No. 198, 1949) and *The Menehune of Polynesia and Other Mythical Little People of Oceania* (Honolulu: Bishop Museum Bulletin No. 203, 1951).

[5] WILLIAM HYDE RICE. *Hawaiian Legends.* Honolulu: Bishop Museum Bulletin No. 3, 1923; New York: Kraus, 1971.

William Hyde Rice (1846–1924) was born of missionary stock at Punahou, Honolulu, where his parents were teachers at the school established there in 1841 (see No. 33). The family moved in 1854 to Lihue on the island of Kauai, where the greater part of his life was spent. Here his chief companions were Hawaiian boys, from whom he readily learned the language. As stated in the preface of the volume, "In fact, until he was twenty, he never *thought* in English, but always in Hawaiian, translating mentally into his mother tongue." Rice attended Oahu College, Punahou, and Braton's College in Oakland, California. He served the kingdom of Hawaii as a member of the House of Representatives for eight years and as a member of the Senate for three years. He took an active part in getting King Kalakaua to sign the constitution of 1887, and was governor of Kauai under Queen Liliuokalani until after the revolution of 1893.

For some years Rice collected and translated the folk tales of old Hawaii that he had heard in his youth. Unfortunately, he did not put any of these legends into print until 1923, when he was urged to do so by his friends and the director of the Bishop Museum. Only some two dozen legends appear in the book, a number of them in shortened form. He tried to make his translations as literal as possible in order to retain the flavor, rhythm, and spirit of the original Hawaiian. He succeeds in making his versions more readable and authentic than those of rival translators. Especially successful is his version of the legend of the menehune, a tribe of busy gnomes whose labors are frequently recorded in the ancient lore of Kauai.

[6] WILLIAM CHICKERING. *Within the Sound of These Waves.* New York: Harcourt, Brace, 1941; Westport, Conn.: Greenwood, 1971.

A history of the leading personalities of the Big Island in early times is given in a chatty style in this book by a Californian who found peace and contentment on those shores. The adventures of such rulers as the legendary Liloa, Hakau, Umi, Lono, and Alapai are given, and the story is continued through the visits of James Cook and George Vancouver up to the death of Kamehameha II.

As the author says, "The first section of this book is a combination of early legends from which I chose what seemed to me the most logical sequence and detail of events. For the second and third sections I used Hawaiian sources also, but for the most part relied on the written evidence of the various mariners and missionaries who visited the islands." At times the style is somewhat racy; for example, speaking of Lono: "while he had mastered the arts of argumentation and conversation and the lore of his people's religion, he was not sure of his left hook."

William Chickering (1916–1945) was born in Piedmont, California, and after graduating from Yale University passed through Hawaii on his way to see the world. Before he reached Manila, however, he decided that he would never see any place he liked so well as Hawaii, and returned to set-

"The King's younger brother hit a mark at thirty yards." Drawing by John Kelly from William Chickering's book on the early history of the Big Island.

tle there. In 1939, in the course of gathering material for an advertising agency, he began to write *Within the Sound of These Waves,* his only book. After the 1941 attack on Pearl Harbor he joined the *Time-Life* staff as a war correspondent, and was killed during a bombing attack on the U.S.S. *New Mexico* in 1945, in Lingayen Gulf in the Philippines. A brief biography by John W. Vandercook appears in the foreword of Chickering's *Letters from the Pacific* (San Francisco: 300 copies privately printed, 1964).

[7] JAMES J. JARVES. *Kiana: A Tradition of Hawaii.* Boston and Cambridge: James Monroe, 1857; London: S. Low, 1857.

James Jackson Jarves (1818–1888), termed by Harold W. Bradley (see Appendix A) "the ablest of the nineteenth-century historians of the islands," was not only the earliest haole historian of Hawaii but also an editor, sketch writer, and the author of the first novel with a Hawaiian setting.

Born in Boston, son of the well-known manufacturer of "Sandwich glass," young Jarves arrived in Hawaii at the age of nineteen, in pursuit of health and recreation. He returned the same year to Boston, to marry his childhood sweetheart and bring her back to Hawaii to share the life of a planter, merchant, and newspaper editor. *The Polynesian,* a weekly, was founded by Jarves in June 1840. Publication was suspended in 1842 when he returned to Boston to see through the press his *History* and an accompanying volume of essays. In May 1844, he was back in Honolulu and resumed publication of *The Polynesian,* which had become the official journal of the royal government. He left Hawaii for the last time early in 1848, but served the kingdom in Washington, D.C., on December 6, 1849, by signing, as a special commissioner, a treaty with the United States government that recognized Hawaiian independence.

The History of the Hawaiian or Sandwich Islands . . . (Boston: Tappan & Dennet, 1843; London: E. Moxon, 1843) was reprinted in 1844, 1847, and 1872. It usually appeared with twenty-five illustrations, some of them drawn from John Webber and Louis Choris. Documentary materials are to be found in seven appendixes. His main acknowledged authorities are the Reverend William Ellis (see No. 24) and *Ka Moolelo Hawaii* (see No. 2), translated by the Reverend Reuben Tinker. The style of the *History* is straightforward and factual, but the volume contains a number of personal observations and amusing incidents.

The second book by Jarves, actually a companion work to the *History,* is *Scenes and Scenery in the Hawaiian Islands . . .* (Boston: James Monroe, 1843). It fulfilled a promise in the preface of the *History* to present an additional volume "which, without being connected with the present, will give in detail all that is necessary to form a correct view of the Hawaiian Islands, their condition, prospects, the every-day concerns of the people, and missionary life as it now exists; the two to form a succinct whole, illustrating each other." The *Scenes* cover four years of living and traveling in the islands. Especially good are the author's descriptions of Kauai, where he had tried and failed to make a success of raising silkworms at Koloa.

Jarves was a pioneer not only in Hawaiian history and journalism but also in the novel with a Hawaiian setting. *Kiana: A Tradition of Hawaii* was not completed until 1856 in Florence, Italy, but was based on a fiction serial that had run in *The Polynesian* in 1841 in six installments. The story is a vehicle for history, pseudo-history, and a good deal of moralizing. In his preface, Jarves cites a legend concerning the arrival of a white priest in Hawaii in the ancient reign of Kiana, and states as well that a vessel was wrecked on Oahu and its captain and his sister were adopted by the chiefs.

The novel, reflecting the author's interest in Mexico as well as Hawaii, opens with the landing, after the wreck, of Captain Juan Alvirez; his beautiful blonde sister, Beatriz; Olmeda, a Dominican monk; and a Mexican Indian captive, Tolta, villain of the plot. These survivors enter a village emptied by a festival of the god Lono. When the Hawaiians return, led by the noble chief Kiana, Alvirez is accepted as an avatar of Lono—as was Captain James Cook on his arrival in the islands. The subsequent story is typical of the nineteenth-century romance, but is not a bad effort, considering that it is the prototype of the modern historical novel with setting in ancient Hawaii.

The chief rival of Jarves in early historical fiction of Hawaii was Charles Martin Newell (1823–1900), whaling captain and physician, who visited the islands a number of times. *Kalani of Oahu* (Boston: published by the author) appeared in 1881. Its hero, the young chief Kalanikapule, offends the goddess Pele and as a result his island is conquered by Kamehameha the Great at the famed battle of Nuuanu

Pali in 1795. Both Kalani, the youthful "king," and his bride, one of Kamehameha's daughters, are killed in the fight.

Under the pseudonym of Captain Bill Barnacle, Newell published *Pehe Nu-e: The Tiger Whale of the Pacific* (Boston: D. Lothrop, 1877), in which appears a battle-scarred whale called by sailors "Mocha Dick"; the influence of Herman Melville's *Moby Dick* is apparent. *Kamehameha, The Conquering King* (New York and London: Putnam) by Newell appeared in 1885; it is a fictional biography of "the Napoleon of the Pacific." The new century was ushered in with *Kelea, The Surf Rider: A Romance of Pagan Hawaii* (New York: Fords, Howard & Hulbert, 1900) by Alexander Stevenson Twombly, which drew upon pre-Cook history gathered by the author during a stay in the republic of Hawaii in 1894.

[8] RALPH S. KUYKENDALL. *The Hawaiian Kingdom.* Vol. I: *Foundation and Transformation.* Honolulu: University of Hawaii, 1938; reprinted University of Hawaii Press, 1947. Vol. II: *Twenty Critical Years.* 1953. Vol. III: *The Kalakaua Dynasty.* 1967. Illus.

Foremost documentary historian of Hawaii, Ralph Simpson Kuykendall (1885–1963) spent forty years engaged in research and writing about island events. He was concerned in particular with the story of the Polynesian realm that preceded the arrival of Captain James Cook and ended with a bloodless revolution in 1893 and the formation of a republic anticipating annexation by the United States.

Kuykendall's monumental three-volume history of the kingdom was the work of a scrupulous and untiring researcher using monographs, contemporary newspapers and periodicals, and documents found in various parts of the world. Trained as a graduate student among the group of historians at Berkeley who were concerned with links between Spanish expansion in the New World and the growth of western

America, Kuykendall extended this interest into the North Pacific, and considered international influences on Hawaii.

Volume one of the series runs to more than four hundred pages, beginning with "a glimpse of ancient Hawaii" before relating the coming of foreigners to the island scene. Other chapters are devoted to the first two Kamehamehas and to early commercial and religious developments. The remaining dozen chapters cover the lengthy reign of Kamehameha III up to his death in 1854. Special aspects treated at length include the beginnings of constitutional government, the development of industries and agriculture, the long struggle for recognition of the independence of the kingdom, continued religious and educational progress, and the land revolution called the Great Mahele.

Volume two covers the second stage of the kingdom, the reigns of the two brothers, Alexander Liholiho (1854–63) and Lot Kamehameha (1863–72). The noteworthy changes during this critical "middle period" receive the attention they deserve. These include developments in transportation, foreign relations, "the life of the land," further constitutional alterations, the decline of whaling and the rise of a sugar economy, the beginnings of labor importation, and the brief reign of William Charles Lunalilo, first elected monarch.

Volume three, by far the most lengthy, begins with the accession of David Kalakaua, the "merry monarch," in 1874 and ends with the tumultuous rule of his sister and successor, Queen Liliuokalani (see No. 40), which culminated in the revolution of 1893. More than seven hundred pages are taken up with events of this latest period of the kingdom. The final chapter, which deals with the revolution, was left unfinished in 1963, and was completed by Charles H. Hunter, who also checked the proofs, collected and labeled the illustrations, and compiled the index. The body of this volume opens with the accession of Kalakaua after a stormy election. Four chapters emphasize the effects of the treaty of reciprocity with the United States that made inevitable the eventual annexation of the islands. Others follow the tangled and often corrupt politics of the reign, the journey of Kalakaua around the world, the fiasco of the Gibson-inspired attempt to obtain the "primacy of the Pacific," the "Bayonet Constitution" and the decline of the Reform Cabinet, and the death of the king in 1891. Four concluding chapters describe the brief reign of Liliuokalani and the final annexation of the Territory of Hawaii under the Stars and Stripes.

Kuykendall's history falls into the realms of political, economic, diplomatic, and general narrative. However, along the way, he includes many items of social and cultural significance. Unfortunately, his death prevented the completion of a planned chapter on the social and cultural history of the monarchy.

The style of Kuykendall's books is scholarly but far from dry, and by means of liberal use of footnotes he can stick to the main argument without distracting digressions. His material is arranged in logical fashion, so that the pages can be used for reference as well as continuous reading.

Kuykendall, a native of California, received a bachelor's degree from the College of the Pacific in 1910 and a master's degree in history from the University of California at Berkeley in 1921. While conducting research for his doctorate in Seville, Spain, he was invited to become executive secretary of the Historical Commission of Hawaii. The first result of his research efforts was an elementary textbook, *A History of Hawaii* (New York: Macmillan, 1940), with introductory chapters by Herbert E. Gregory. When the duties of the Commission—which also involved the investigation and preservation of objects and places of interest in Hawaii—were taken over by the University of Hawaii in 1932, Kuykendall became an assistant professor of history. Thereafter, until his death in 1963, he served on the faculty, and worked at his desk in the library even after he became an emeritus professor in 1950. In 1956 he was awarded an honorary doctorate of humane letters, in recognition of his lifetime of research in island history. He was co-author with L. T. Gill of *Hawaii in the World War* (Honolulu: Historical Commission, 1928). He collaborated with A. Grove Day on the one-volume textbook, *Hawaii, A History* (New York: Prentice-

Hall, 1948), which was revised in 1961 after Hawaii became a state. Kuykendall published some fifty historical articles and pamphlets, and was always willing to drop his labors and discuss his wide-ranging interests with callers. His massive history of the Hawaiian Kingdom is a storehouse of basic information for generations of historians to come.

[9] JAMES COOK. *The Journals of Captain James Cook on His Voyages of Discovery*. Edited by J. C. Beaglehole. 3 vol. and portfolio. London: Hakluyt Society, 1955, 1961, 1967.

Leader of the expedition that first revealed the existence of the Hawaiian islands to the outside world, James Cook (1728–1779) was destined to lose his life on a Big Island shore, through a misunderstanding with the people who had accepted him as one of their gods, returned to bring them valuable goods from overseas.

Captain Cook was greeted by the Hawaiians as their ancient god Lono. Unaware of the consequences of his deification, Cook agreed to undergo a ritual on the temple platform at Kealakekua Bay.

The world's greatest explorer by sea, who was to spend the last decade of his life charting the Pacific from the Antarctic to the Arctic Circles, was born in a farm cottage in Yorkshire. He sailed the North Sea before rising to the rank of master's mate in the Royal Navy, then served during the battle for Quebec, and for four years mapped the coasts of Newfoundland. With the rank of lieutenant, he was chosen to head the *Endeavour* expedition (1768–71), which observed at Tahiti the transit of the planet Venus across the face of the sun. The next six months he spent mapping the coasts of New Zealand and the eastern side of Australia, which he named New South Wales. Escaping a perilous grounding on a part of the Great Barrier Reef, Cook brought his vessel to Batavia and thence back to England on his historic first voyage.

During his second voyage, in command of the *Resolution* and *Adventure,* Cook was the first to sail south of the Antarctic Circle, and proved that the suppositious continent of Terra Australis Incognita must be limited to the area of present-day Antarctica. He visited parts of the group now called the Cook Islands, discovered Tonga (which he called the Friendly Islands), New Caledonia, and Norfolk Island, and rediscovered Easter Island and the Marquesas group. The *Adventure,* under Tobias Furneaux, separated from her consort and reached home a full year before Cook's *Resolution,* which returned to England in July 1775, having sailed more than sixty thousand miles in a voyage lasting more than three years—the longest voyage then on record. Thanks to Cook's anticipation of the need for vitamins in diet, not one of his crew died of scurvy.

Cook was called a third time to sail into the Pacific. In July 1776—the month that the American colonies declared their independence from Great Britain—two ships, the *Resolution* and the *Discovery,* left Plymouth on another round-the-world voyage. Cook was ordered to repatriate Omai, a native of the island of Huahine in the Society group, who had been taken to England by Furneaux, and to explore a western entrance to the "Northwest Passage" that might enable him to sail through an ice-free route from the North Pacific to the North Atlantic.

Wearing masking helmets of gourds, Hawaiian warriors paddle a canoe in the waters of Kealakekua Bay, site of the death of Captain James Cook.

Heading northward, on January 18, 1778, the two ships sighted an island to the northeast and, soon after, another to the north. Next day, another was seen to the northwest. These were Oahu, Kauai, and Niihau, westernmost of the main islands of the Hawaiian group, which Cook christened the Sandwich Islands in honor of his noble patron in the Admiralty.

After trading with the Hawaiian inhabitants, who spoke a Polynesian dialect similar to that of the Tahitians on board his ship, Cook charted the Oregon coast and then spent almost a year mapping parts of Alaska and the Bering Sea. In the Arctic he recalled the warm Sandwich Islands and returned there to spend the winter. He discovered the southern group, sighting Maui on November 26, 1778, and later glimpsing Molokai. The ships spent six weeks rounding the largest island, Hawaii, until they found anchorage at Kealakekua Bay on the west shore, where ten thousand Hawaiians greeted Cook as their ancient god Lono, returning to them in the harvest season of makahiki. The people offered supplies to their incarnated deity, but the old Polynesian habit of "borrowing" the property of others led to conflicts. When the ships were forced to return to Kealakekua to repair a damaged mast, the mood of the Hawaiians had changed and the theft of Cook's boat led to his incursion ashore in an attempt to secure hostages. His death on the beach, and burial in the waters of the archipelago that his ships were to make known to the rest of the world was a personal as well as a national tragedy. Thereafter, the "Sandwich Islands" were to be included in the far-ranging trade of the thriving British Empire.

The official account of the third voyage is that of James Cook and James King, *Voyage to the Pacific Ocean . . . for Making Discoveries in the Northern Hemisphere* . . . 3 vol. (London: printed by W. & A. Strahan for G. Nicol & T. Cadell, 1784). The first two of these volumes were written by Cook himself; after his death on February 14, 1779, the work was continued by his successor in command of the *Resolution,* James King. The book was frequently reprinted and widely translated. It was, however, anticipated by four unofficial volumes by members of the expedition. A German foremast hand, Heinrich Zimmermann, issued a book at Mannheim in 1781, of which two English translations have been made—*Account of the Third Voyage of Captain Cook, 1776–80,* by U. Tewsley (Wellington, N.Z.: W. A. G. Skinner, 1926) and *Zimmermann's Captain Cook,* by F. W. Howay (Toronto: Ryerson Press, 1930). John Rickman, second lieutenant of the *Discovery,* published *Journal of Captain Cook's Last Voyage to the Pacific Ocean* . . . (London: E. Newbury, 1781). William Ellis, surgeon's second mate, published *An Authentic Narrative of a Voyage Performed by Captain Cook and Captain Clerke* . . . 2 vol. (London: printed for G. Robinson, J. Sewell & J. Debrett, 1782). The book by John Ledyard, American corporal of marines, *A Journal of Captain Cook's Last Voyage to the Pacific Ocean* (Hartford, Conn.: Nathaniel Patten, 1783), was based heavily on Rickman. A valuable contribution by a skilled writer, David Samwell, surgeon of the *Discovery,* is *A Narrative of the Death of Captain Cook* . . . (London: G. G. J. and J.

Robinson, 1786), which appeared after the official account. Some of the many books about Cook's exploits are listed on pages 40–41 in *Pacific Islands Literature* by A. Grove Day (Honolulu: University Press of Hawaii, 1971). Two novels about Cook in Hawaii are *Lost Eden* by Paul McGinnis (New York: McBride, 1947; London: Quality Press, 1953), an authentic first-person story of a young Englishman who deserts in Hawaii and lives ashore; and *The Return of Lono* (Boston: Little, Brown, 1956) by O. A. Bushnell (see No. 32).

[10] GAVAN DAWS. *Shoal of Time: A History of the Hawaiian Islands.* New York: Macmillan, 1968; (paperback) Honolulu: University Press of Hawaii, 1974.

Several one-volume histories of the Hawaiian Islands have been issued for the adult reader in recent years. The most outstanding is that by Alan Gavan Daws, an Australian born in 1933 who came to study and teach at the University of Hawaii in 1958.

Shoal of Time opens with the arrival of Captain James Cook in 1778 and culminates with Hawaii's admission to statehood in 1959. Between these dates the author unfolds in entertaining style the major and minor episodes of island history and presents a pageant of Hawaiian chiefs and monarchs; white traders, whalers, and missionaries; plantation owners and Oriental immigrants; diplomatic agents and revolutionaries; and labor leaders who organized the agricultural and dock workers according to mainland patterns after World War II. The work is extensively footnoted and is based on a lengthy bibliography of obscure as well as better-known sources. The attitude is sympathetic to those that Daws considers underprivileged; the tone is sometimes sarcastic and often the personages appear to be amusing puppets of fate.

Daws left Hawaii in 1975 to hold the chair of Pacific History at the Australian National University, Canberra. He is also author of *Holy Man: Father Damien of Molokai* (New York: Harper, 1973), a well-researched and objective, illustrated biography of the Catholic priest who ended his labors in the leper settlement.

Other authors have written one-volume histories. An earlier one by A. Grove Day, attempting to present the main course of history with social sidelights, is *Hawaii and Its People* (New York: Duell, Sloan & Pearce, 1955, 1960, 1969). This book was based partly on the author's previous collaboration with Ralph S. Kuykendall on a one-volume work, *Hawaii: A History* (see No. 8), which for some years was used as a text at the University of Hawaii.

Hawaii: An Informal History by Gerrit P. Judd (paperback, New York: Crowell-Collier, 1961) is a chatty narrative by a descendant of the missionary Judd family.

The Islands by W. Storrs Lee (New York: Holt, 1966) is a popular account by a former dean of Middlebury College.

Hawaii, An Uncommon History by Edward Joesting (New York: W. W. Norton, 1972) is "uncommon" mainly because it tells the island story with special attention to the personalities of varied and sometimes little known participants. Many details are drawn from biographies and newspaper items. Joesting, born in St. Paul, Minnesota, in 1925, took a leave from his position as an executive with one of the "Big Five" companies to prepare this highly readable volume.

[11] A. GROVE DAY and **CARL STROVEN (eds.).** *A Hawaiian Reader.* New York: Appleton-Century-Crofts, 1959; Popular Library, 1961.

In the year of statehood appeared the first anthology of the literature of Hawaii, containing thirty-seven selections from the writings of thirty authors, including Hiram Bingham, Mark Twain, Robert Louis Stevenson, Jack London, Genevieve Taggard, W. Somerset Maugham, and James Jones. In his introduction James Michener wrote about the editors: "They are without question the two men best qualified in the entire world to edit this particular book. . . . Rarely has a man writing the foreword of a book done so with more pleasure than I feel in presenting this work to the public. It is as good as it could possibly be.'' The collection is still available, after almost twenty years, in paperback form.

Ten years previously, Stroven and Day had published *The Spell of the Pacific: An Anthology of Its Literature* (New York: Macmillan, 1949), also with an introduction by Michener. It included some two hundred pages of writing from Hawaii. Almost two decades later these editors issued *The Spell of Hawaii* (New York: Meredith Press, 1968), a companion volume to *A Hawaiian Reader,* containing twenty-four equally impressive selections. Day and Stroven also edited two other anthologies from the Pacific area: *Best South Sea Stories* and *True Tales of the South Seas* (New York: Appleton-Century, 1964; 1966).

Carl Stroven, born in 1901 in California, served for forty years at the University of Hawaii as professor of English and university librarian. His Stanford University classmate, A. Grove Day, born in 1904 in Pennsylvania, served for twenty-five years at the same university. Together, they taught over the years a unique course, ''Literature of the Pacific,'' inaugurated by Stroven in 1936.

Two other anthologies of Hawaiiana appeared with the same date of publication. *A Hawaiian Anthology,* edited by Gerrit P. Judd IV (New York: Macmillan, 1967), contains three sections: ''Hawaii's History,'' ''Hawaiian Traditions and Places,'' and ''Hawaii in Literature.'' The last section comprises pages from Mark Twain's *Roughing It,* ''The Bottle Imp'' by Robert Louis Stevenson, and ''The Water Baby'' by Jack London. The editor's purpose, as stated, ''has simply been to give a broad sample of the innumerable writings which deal with the Hawaiian experience.''

Hawaii: A Literary Chronicle, edited by W. Storrs Lee (New York: Funk & Wagnalls, 1967, with illustrations by W. Ralph Merrill), attempts to narrate the history of the islands by means of more than fifty selections, linked by commentary. ''This is not an anthology in the ordinary sense,'' the editor states. "The book has sequence and continuity; it tells a chronological story; it is intended to be read from the beginning, not given the dip-and-dabble treatment accorded most anthologies." Not all the many authors quoted are literary figures, and some did not visit Hawaii.

In comparison with many states of the Union, Hawaii is quite competently represented by selections from authors who have written about the scene and its people.

[12] **MARY KAWENA PUKUI** and **ALFONS L. KORN.** *The Echo of Our Song: Chants and Poems of the Hawaiians.* Honolulu: University Press of Hawaii, 1973.

From earliest times, the chanting of poetry enabled the Hawaiians to celebrate ritually the beauty of their islands, the abundance of creatures of nature, the majesty of their rulers, and the deeds of their heroes and deities. Despite the impact of foreign culture, many of the older chants have survived, and others continue to be shaped to commemorate various occasions or to accompany a dance.

The best collection of native Hawaiian poetry was translated and edited by Mary K. Pukui and Alfons L. Korn in *The Echo of Our Song.* Twenty-nine chants and poems, with Hawaiian texts and translations, reflect a wide range of styles from both ancient and post-missionary times. An appendix explicates a number of the selections and makes valuable comments.

Mary Kawena Pukui, of Samoan, Hawaiian, and New England ancestry, was born in 1895 on the island of Hawaii. In the 1920s she began working with Laura C. S. Green, born in 1864 at Makawao, Maui, daughter of a missionary family. Green is listed as author of three volumes of stories, tales, and sayings published at Poughkeepsie, New York, by Martha Beckwith (see No. 1), under the titles of *Hawaiian Stories and Wise Sayings* (1923); *Folk-tales from Hawaii* (1926); and *Legends of Kawelo* (1929). The majority of the legends in the first two books were contributions of Pukui; the legend of

"Let the echo of our song be heard" was the plea of many nineteenth-century poets among the people of Hawaii.

Kawelo was dictated to Napoleon K. Pukui by an old Hawaiian. Pukui was acknowledged as author of a fourth volume, *Hawaiian Folk Tales* (Poughkeepsie, 1933). She worked for years as a translator of many historical documents at the Bernice P. Bishop Museum and was senior author with Samuel H. Elbert of the *Hawaiian Dictionary* (Honolulu: University of Hawaii Press, 1957, 1971) and, with Elbert and Esther T. Mookini, of *Place Names of Hawaii* (revised and enlarged edition, Honolulu: University Press of Hawaii, 1974; first published 1966). A paperback abridgment of the *Dictionary,* by Pukui, Elbert, and Mookini, was published by the University Press of Hawaii in 1975.

Korn, co-translator of *The Echo of Our Song,* is author of *The Victorian Visitors* (see No. 34) and has contributed various articles on Hawaiian history and literature.

Another important source of lyrics is *Na Mele o Hawai'i Nei: One Hundred and One Hawaiian Songs* (Honolulu: University of Hawaii Press, 1970), a collection by Samuel H. Elbert and Noelani K. Mahoe, with authoritative texts and translations, notes on the composers, comments on poetic vocabulary, and an analysis of structure and symbolism; music is not included.

[13] GEORGE VANCOUVER. *Voyage of Discovery to the North Pacific Ocean and Round the World in the Years 1790–95* . . . . 3 vol. and atlas. Illus. London: C. J. and J. Robinson, J. Edwards, 1798.

George Vancouver (1758–98) was a highly competent naval officer who served under James Cook during Cook's last two voyages, and later made a celebrated name for himself in Pacific discovery.

Entering the British Navy at the age of thirteen, Vancouver acted as able seaman on board the *Resolution* on Cook's second Pacific voyage and as midshipman on the *Discovery* on Cook's third voyage. After attaining the rank of lieutenant, he saw action in the West Indies. In September 1789, he was appointed to head an exploring expedition to the South Seas in command of a new vessel, also named *Discovery,* to repossess the fur-rich Nootka Sound region from Spain and to seek the Northwest Passage. After settling the Nootka dispute, Vancouver discovered the Gulf of Georgia north of Puget Sound and circled the large island now bearing his name. While working for two years charting and naming the coasts and inlets north of San Francisco, he and his crews spent three winters in the Hawaiian group.

Vancouver was the most important visitor to the islands during the reign of Kamehameha I, and gave a number of valuable descriptions of the monarch and his court. The pair did not meet during the Englishman's first stop, in March 1792, but on successive visits, in the spring of 1793 and that of 1794, he saw all the islands and became well acquainted with their people. On the second visit the ships introduced cattle and sheep, as well as goats and geese. At this time Vancouver met Kaahumanu, favorite wife of Kamehameha. When he returned the following year, he learned that the pair were separated because the king suspected her of dalliance

English seamen view the heights of Mount Hualalai during a visit to the Big Island by the expedition of George Vancouver.

with a handsome chief named Kaiana. By a clever strategem, Vancouver was able to reunite the estranged pair.

In 1793, Vancouver fitted out one of Kamehameha's double canoes with a full set of sails, and gave him a Union Jack to fly before his house. The following year, he helped the king's carpenter to finish building a sailing ship, which was christened the *Britannia*. However, the British captain spoke out violently against the trade in arms and ammunition that soulless foreign shipmen were carrying on, selling defective guns and adulterated powder to warring chiefs. Just before his final departure from Hawaii, Vancouver obtained from Kamehameha what the Englishman called a "cession" of the Big Island to Great Britian. His government never ratified the agreement; nevertheless, England's influence was foremost in the islands in the early years.

The *Discovery* returned to England by way of Cape Horn and arrived in the Thames in October 1795. In ill health,

Vancouver spent the remaining months of his life preparing his journals for publication. He had corrected the proofs of all but the last few pages of his work when he died in May 1798. The adventures of the men of the *Discovery,* along with those of the tender *Chatham* and the store ship *Daedalus,* are a stirring part of Hawaiian history, which Vancouver relates in flowing style.

A biography of this Pacific explorer is *Surveyor of the Sea* by Bern Anderson (Seattle, Wash.: University of Washington Press, 1960).

[14] ARCHIBALD CAMPBELL. *Voyage Round the World, from 1806 to 1812.* Edinburgh: A. Constable, 1816; Honolulu: University of Hawaii Press, 1967.

A minor classic among narratives of the sea as well as a primary source of information about life in early Hawaii before the coming of the missionaries is Archibald Campbell's *Voyage.* Born near Glasgow around 1787, Campbell received "the common rudiments of education," served as a weaver's apprentice, and ran away to sea at the age of fourteen. After making several voyages to various parts of the world, he joined the American ship *Eclipse,* bound for the Russian outposts at Kamchatka and the Aleutian Islands. The ship was wrecked on a reef off the Alaskan coast, and while Campbell was attempting to get help from the nearest Russian settlement, both his feet were frozen and later had to be amputated. A returning ship carried him to Hawaii, where he was taken into the household of King Kamehameha the Great, to be the royal sailmaker. In this capacity he remained for more than a year, in 1809 and part of 1810.

Historians are indebted to Campbell for a number of lively descriptions of Kamehameha I at the height of his powers as a ruler of his people, employer of white residents in the islands, and shrewd trader with visiting ship captains. He pictures the king working in a taro patch to give an example to his subjects, as well as playing the native game of konane and risking his life dodging spears thrown by his warriors during the annual makahiki ritual. Campbell also gives good accounts of native customs around 1810, seen from the point of view of a wandering Scotsman. One of the appendixes of this book gives a glossary of Hawaiian words.

Making his way home after further adventures in South America, Campbell earned a meager living playing the violin for the amusement of steamboat passengers on the River Clyde until he published his book, which sold unusually well. With the proceeds, he went to New York and started a small chandlery business, continuing there at least until 1821, when all trace of him disappears. A novel based on his adventures is *The Restless Voyage* (New York: Prentice-Hall, 1948; London: Harrap, 1950), by Stanley D. Porteus.

[15] OTTO VON KOTZEBUE. *A Voyage of Discovery into the South Sea and Beering's Straits, for the Purpose of Exploring a North-East Passage* . . . . Translated from the German by H. E. Lloyd. 3 vol. London: Longman, Hurst, Rees, Orme & Brown, 1821.

Otto von Kotzebue (1787–1846), a Baltic German and Russian subject, devoted the best years of his life to service in the Russian Imperial Navy, which at that time was expanding into the Pacific. At the age of seventeen, Otto volunteered to sail with his uncle, Adam Johann von Krusenstern, on a circumnavigation in the ship *Nadeshda* (see Appendix A). On this voyage Otto first visited the Hawaiian Islands, in June 1804.

In command of his own ship, *Rurik,* Kotzebue explored the Pacific from 1815 to 1818. The German original of his *Voyage of Discovery* appeared in three volumes at Weimar in 1821, and the English translation came out the same year.

The *Rurik* arrived from California off the island of Hawaii in November 1816. On the staff of the captain were three "scientific gentlemen": Adelbert von Chamisso, botanist and poet, who wrote in German a two-volume account of the voyage; Johann Friedrich Eschscholtz, naturalist; and Ludwig Choris, a young artist whose lovely watercolors give the

Hawaiian warriors perform a hula dance in honor of the arrival in 1816 of the Russian warship *Rurik,* commanded by Otto von Kotzebue.

best views of the people and places of Hawaii during the reign of Kamehameha. Choris drew the first portraits of this first king of the islands. The Russians, off Kailua on the Kona Coast, found that Kamehameha had stationed four hundred warriors, armed with muskets, to defend the beach from what the king considered an invading warship. Kotzebue then learned that a German filibuster, Dr. Georg Anton Scheffer, had brought Russian troops to the island of Kauai, had encouraged King Kaumualii of that island to become a subject of the Czar, and had flown the Russian flag over a fort built at Waimea.

Kotzebue hastily disavowed any knowledge of the Scheffer incursion, and he and his gentlemen were regally received on November 24 outside the straw "palace" of Kamehameha. The crew of the *Rurik* sailed that night for Oahu after a red-letter day ashore, but Scheffer and his cohorts were not evicted from their hold on Kauai until the following May.

On his third visit to the islands, Captain Kotzebue arrived

in Honolulu late in 1824, in command of the ship *Predpiatie.* The English version of the two-volume German account is entitled *A New Voyage Round the World . . .* (London: H. Colburn & R. Bentley, 1830). On this circumnavigation, the Russians explored various Pacific groups, including the Societies, the Tuamotus, Samoa, the Marshalls, the Philippines, and Hawaii. In Honolulu, Kotzebue was received by such earlier acquaintances as Governor Kinau and the queen dowager, Namahana—of whose visit to the ship he gives a delightful description. Namahana was among the first of the great chiefs to accept the Christianity dispensed by the New England missionaries, who had established themselves between the visits of the *Rurik* and the *Predpiatie.* Kotzebue was not pleased with the pious atmosphere he found in the islands at this time, and wrote sarcastically: "The streets, formerly so full of life and animation, are now deserted; games of all kinds, even the most innocent, are sternly prohibited; singing is a punishable offense; and the consummate profligacy of attempting to dance would certainly find no mercy."

Kotzebue was the son of the famed German playwright who has been called "perhaps the strongest single influence on the development of European drama," and is the most graphic and entertaining writer among the many Russian explorers of the Pacific (between 1803 and 1849 there were thirty-six round-the-world Russian voyages, most of them following the pioneer track of Krusenstern). The last captain of a Russian warship to interview Kamehameha I was V. M. Golovnin of the sloop *Kamchatka,* on his way in the autumn of 1818 to investigate the declining Russian American Company at its headquarters at Sitka, Alaska.

[16] DARWIN TEILHET. *The Mission of Jeffery Tolamy.* New York: William Sloane Associates, 1951.

Darwin Teilhet, a novelist, wrote several books about the Hawaiian Islands, which he found a fertile setting for lively fiction.

In *The Mission of Jeffery Tolamy,* Teilhet showed his skill in historical re-creation of the 1816 period, a time when a Russian filibustering expedition attempted to annex the Hawaiian archipelago to Czar Alexander's empire. Tolamy, a young Pennsylvanian who had learned to speak some Hawaiian from a native hospital-mate, is sent by James Monroe as a secret agent on an American ship, laden with munitions, to help the Hawaiian rulers defend themselves against a suspected British attempt to seize the islands. Instead, he finds himself faced with the prospect of a Russian takeover, led by the sinister figure of Dr. Georg Anton Scheffer, a German adventurer backed by the governor of Russian Alaska.

One challenging episode after another engages Tolamy's efforts during the year—part of which he spends in a dungeon under the Russian fort on the Waimea River on the island of Kauai. He meets all the principal chiefs and foreigners in the islands at the time, including Governor John Young, Prime Minister Kalanimoku ("Billy Pitt"), King Kamehameha of Hawaii, and King Kaumualii of Kauai. Sally Partridge, daughter of a trader, is alienated from Jeffery by a series of misunderstandings. Jeffery becomes a key figure in the forcible eviction of the Russians when he discovers that his Hawaiian hospital-mate was Prince George Kaumualii, son of the king of Kauai, who believed his heir had died years earlier. Suspense keeps the fictional pot bubbling, and the characterization is stronger than in the usual novel of adventure.

In his "Historical Note," Teilhet discusses his factual sources on the Russian episode and states that, with the exception of Captain Sam Crowell, Ben Partridge, and his daughter Sally—three who were invented "to give Jeffery an emotional interior and reality in his own right"—all the characters are drawn from history. He differs with modern historians in assuming that Captain Otto von Kotzebue (see No. 15) was aware of the Scheffer conspiracy when Kotzebue's ship *Rurik* visited Kamehameha at Kailua in November 1816, but the events of the story do not conflict with fact beyond the usual license of the historical novelist. A recent, brief, factual account of the Scheffer episode can be found in chapter one of *Adventurers of the Pacific* by A. Grove Day (New York: Meredith, 1969).

A year previously, Teilhet published a novel of contemporary Hawaii, *The Happy Island* (New York: William Sloane Associates, 1950). The story concerns Parker Mattison, who had been with a cloak-and-dagger outfit in World War II and, under the guise of being a modernist painter living on an island resembling Maui, was actually part of an undercover organization aimed at averting labor difficulties among the pineapple workers. The island is controlled, by means of a variety of covert arrangements, by the baronial E. P. Tothic, head of a large plantation complex. Mattison's role in aborting a costly strike conflicts with his love for Laina, a beautiful part-Hawaiian girl from Kauai who has come to live with him and who represents the spirit of modern young Hawaii of the post-1945 period.

Darwin L. Teilhet (1904–1964), born at Wyanette, Illinois, collaborated frequently with his wife, Hildegarde Tolman Teilhet; both were graduates of Stanford University, California. One of their joint works is *The Feather Cloak Murders* (New York: Sloane, 1936), a detective novel of Hawaii featuring Baron von Kaz. Teilhet wrote stories for young people under the pseudonym of "Cyrus Fisher"; one of these is *The Hawaiian Sword,* based on old accounts that when Captain Cook landed, he was shown a sword of iron, although the natives did not possess this metal.

[17] JAMES A. MICHENER. *Hawaii.* New York: Random House, 1959.

Many readers, especially outside the state of Hawaii, are aware of only one novel about the islands—Michener's giant volume that appeared in 1959, the year that Hawaii joined the sisterhood of American states. This tidal-wave of a book is still widely read around the world, and too often its fictional treatment of a social scene is taken as gospel, even by those aware of the actual historic sequence of events.

Michener's *Hawaii,* whatever minor faults it may have, is

on the whole the most compelling novel yet written about the coming of the various peoples to the future fiftieth state. The period covered runs from millions of years ago, before the geologic formation of the chain of islands in the North Pacific, up to 1954. The areas covered extend from China, Japan, and the Philippines through the South Pacific, and reach New England. Dozens of characters throng the pages, representing the varied ethnic groups that were to populate the island stage, bringing with them their own food, their own gods, their own flowers and fruits and concepts. Among several main themes, one is prominent: "paradise" is not a place that a seeker must discover, but a stage that can serve as "a crucible of exploration and development." Faithful to truth if not to fact, *Hawaii* is a dramatic pageant of the intermingling of distinctive social groups over many generations in a fascinating Pacific microcosm. A lengthy discussion of the various aspects of *Hawaii* comprises chapter six of *James A. Michener* (New York: Twayne United States Authors No. 60, 1964; second edition, 1977) by A. Grove Day.

James Albert Michener does not know the names of his parents or the date of his birth. He was picked up as a waif on the streets of Doylestown, Pennsylvania, by a kindly widow who brought him up with her own son. Surviving dire poverty by taking various boyhood jobs, he earned a scholarship to Swarthmore College, and after graduation and travels in Europe he became a professor and editor. Although reared as a Quaker, Michener in 1942 volunteered for combat duty in the Navy. He visited about fifty Pacific islands as part of his aircraft maintenance work; from this experience came his first book, *Tales of the South Pacific* (New York: Macmillan, 1947), which was awarded a Pulitzer Prize the same year. Later volumes about the Pacific include *Return to Paradise* (New York: Random House, 1951) and *Rascals in Paradise* (New York: Random House, 1957) in collaboration with A. Grove Day—a volume that in chapters one, four, and seven covers events in Hawaii.

"Obookiah, a Native of Owhyhee" inspired the first New England mission to the "Sandwich Islands."

[18] HENRY OBOOKIAH. *Memoirs.* Edited by Edwin Dwight. New Haven, Conn.: Religious Intelligencer, 1818; illus. reprint Honolulu: Hawaii Conference of the United Church of Christ, 1968.

Inspiration for the first Christian mission to the Sandwich Islands derived from a slim volume published in 1818 in New England, telling, in the words of an exiled Hawaiian lad and those of his friends, the life and death of a wandering convert.

Opukahaia (the native name means "stomach-cut-open") was renamed "Henry Obookiah" when, orphaned by tribal war, he was taken from the islands in 1809 by Captain Caleb Brintnall in the *Triumph.* He was found weeping on the steps of Yale College in Connecticut because he was ashamed of his ignorance of the world and of the meaning of Christianity. Edwin Dwight and other students volunteered to be Henry's tutors. An eager pupil, Henry was sent to the foreign mission school started at Cornwall, Connecticut. There he started to translate the Bible into Hawaiian—the true pioneer in this endeavor—and yearned to return to his islands as a missionary. He died of typhus fever at the school in February 1818; but a funeral sermon preached by the Reverend Lyman Beecher and the publication of the *Memoirs* in several editions spread a wave of interest that culminated in the sailing of the missionary bark *Thaddeus* the year after his death.

Simply told as the story was, it became a best-seller in New England, and is enjoyable for its own sake as well as for its status as the stimulus for the Hawaii mission.

[19] HIRAM BINGHAM. *A Residence of Twenty-one Years in the Sandwich Islands* . . . . Illus. New York: Sherman Converse, 1847; New York: Praeger, 1969, facsimile of 3rd edition.

The first missionaries to Hawaii arrived in 1820 aboard the brig *Thaddeus,* sent out from Boston by the American Board of Commissioners for Foreign Missions. They came at a time of religious vacuum in the islands. The young King Kamehameha II (Liholiho) and his advisers had just thrown off the old Polynesian creed, with its irksome tabus; and most of his people, bewildered without their many gods, listened willingly to the new teachings.

Foremost among those of the "First Company" on the *Thaddeus* was the Reverend Hiram Bingham (1789–1869), son of a Vermont farmer. A young man with a high forehead and a determination verging upon stubborness, Bingham was destined to spend more than two decades in active mission work in the islands. The chiefs surrounding the king—including Kalanimoku, the prime minister (nicknamed "Billy Pitt"); the queen dowager and regent, Kaahumanu; Governor Boki of Oahu; and many other influential leaders—eagerly heard the Gospel and tried to apply its teachings to

Queen Kaahumanu listens to a sermon by Hiram Bingham at Waimea, Oahu, in 1826. (After a sketch by the Reverend Mr. Bingham.)

their rule over the kingdom. When Liholiho died in England in 1824, he was succeeded by his young brother, Kamehameha III (Kauikeaouli), whose political reforms markedly reflected the ideas of the American mission.

"I have aimed," Bingham says in his preface, "to introduce to my readers the Hawaiian people and their country, with its mountain, valley, and volcanic scenery; their rulers, teachers, friends, and opposers; their habitations, schools, churches, revivals, etc., as they appeared to myself, and to show the footprints of the nation's progress in their uphill efforts to rise amid conflicting influences." A first chapter gives an account of the origin and development of the Hawaiians through the date of the death of Captain Cook. The next covers the forty years following 1779, and the third presents "preparatory measures for planting a Christian mission at the Sandwich Islands, 1809-1819." Then follow annals from 1820 through 1840, the years during which Bingham and his family resided in the islands. A final chapter covers events of the five years 1841–45, after the departure of the Binghams and before the printing of the volume. The book is illustrated with engravings, and concludes with a valuable list of missionaries sent by the American Board between 1819 and 1847. Equally valuable is a prefatory list of names of "the principal Hawaiian personages found in this work," with literal translations of most of these names.

Bingham, born at Bennington, Vermont, worked his father's farm until he came of age, and belatedly graduated from Middlebury College at the age of twenty-six. He spent three more years at Andover Theological Seminary before being accepted for the Hawaii mission. Since the men of the company were required to be married, Hiram sought and found a mate in Sybil Moseley, who happened to attend his ordination at Goshen, Connecticut; they were married a fortnight later. They founded a family still prominent in American affairs, but the Hawaii experience had probably the greatest influence upon the formation of Bingham's career.

Concerning Bingham's book, James A. Michener wrote, in his introduction to *A Hawaiian Reader:* "Hiram Bingham is one of the most difficult great men of history to love, but everyone looking at either Hawaii or the Pacific in general is required either to stand for Bingham, the bigoted Old Testament figure, or for those other Americans who almost destroyed the islands. I have always been for Bingham, and I consider his awkward and unlovely book, *A Residence of Twenty-one Years in the Sandwich Islands,* the most significant volume yet published on the islands."

[20] LUCY GOODALE THURSTON. *The Life and Times of Lucy G. Thurston.* Ann Arbor, Mich.: S. C. Andrews, 1882; Honolulu: The Friend, 1934.

The wife of one of the missionaries of the first company that arrived in the islands in 1820 was born in Marlborough, Massachusetts. Lucy Goodale (1795–1876), daughter of a deacon of the Congregational church, was graduated from Bradford Academy and became a schoolteacher. At twenty-four she married Asa Thurston, a graduate of Yale College and Andover Theological Seminary, newly ordained as a minister and preparing to leave on the brig *Thaddeus* for Hawaii.

After a five-month voyage, the Thurstons settled at Kailua on the island of Hawaii. Unlike many other early mission workers, this couple stayed in the islands, and were responsible for much of the success of the Hawaiian mission. Descendants of the family are still prominent in the state of Hawaii today.

In her old age, with her faculties unimpaired although she was the last surviving member of the original company, Lucy Thurston compiled her memoirs from journals and letters. Her accounts revive the early experiences of the mission, their relations with the chiefs, the harsh punishments for violations of tabus, the rigors of sailing for four days on a native schooner from Honolulu to Lahaina, Hawaiian burial customs, and the graciousness of Queen Regent Kaahumanu to the women of the mission.

Lucy Thurston's remarks are sometimes quite secular, as in her report of the single known instance wherein a European lady was molested by a Hawaiian. It happened in the first year of her work at the Kailua station, when she was in her dwelling, teaching the future King Liholiho: "A pagan priest of the old religion, somewhat intoxicated, entered, and with insolent manners divested himself of his girdle. Before I was aware, every individual had left the house and yard. The priest and I stood face to face, *alone.* As he advanced, I receded. Thus we performed many evolutions around the room. In a retired corner stood a high post bedstead. He threw himself upon the bed and seemed to enjoy the luxury of rolling from side to side upon its white covering. On leaving it he again approached and pursued me with increased eagerness. My tactics were then changed. I went out at one front door, and he after me. I entered the other front door, and he after me. Thus out and in, out and in, we continued to make many circuits. The scene of action was next in the dooryard. There, being nearly entrapped in a corner, having a substantial stick in my hand, I gave the fellow a severe blow across the arm. As he drew back under the smart, I slipped by and escaped. Loss and pain together so enraged him that he picked up clubs and threw them at me. There we parted, without his ever touching me with a finger."

James A. Michener once wrote, concerning this book: "In 1855 Mrs. Lucy Goodale Thurston, a missionary wife then sixty years old, faced sure death from cancer of the breast. With the fortitude that marked all the early missionaries, she held herself in a chair, without sedatives, for an hour and a half, while a surgeon cut away her entire breast. She conversed with him during the operation, and her later account of what happened in those dreadful hours . . . could well serve as the spiritual summary of the missionary."—*A Hawaiian Reader* (New York: Appleton-Century-Crofts, 1959), xv.

[21] ALBERTINE LOOMIS. *Grapes of Canaan.* New York: Dodd, Mead, 1951; (paperback) Honolulu: Hawaiian Mission Children's Society, 1966, as *Grapes of Canaan: Hawaii 1820.*

The "best documentary novel of early Hawaii" was written by a great-granddaughter of Elisha and Maria Loomis, youngest members of the first company of missionaries that landed in Hawaii in 1820. The story, based on the Loomis journals and letters as well as much other research, covers the period from 1820 to 1827, when the Loomis family left to return to New York.

Loomis's original intention, when her exhaustive research in libraries from Washington, D.C. to the Mission Children's Society Library in Honolulu was completed, was to write the usual novel, inventing incidents and characters to fill out the story and cast. But she discovered that no fictionist could dream up a story more thrilling than the bare truth of the events of those pioneer years of the Hawaiian mission. Nor could one create characters more striking than people like Hiram Bingham and Queen Kaahumanu, or American sea captains like "Mad Jack" Percival or Thomas ap Catesby Jones. The result of her work is a charming narrative that can be read with delight and remembered with profit. The appendix identifies a number of personages mentioned in the book and gives a glossary of Hawaiian words.

Loomis is also author of *To All People: A History of the Hawaii Conference of the United Church of Christ* (Honolulu: Hawaii Conference, 1970). The missionary labors of the New England Congregationalists did not cease when Hawaii became a "home mission" in 1863. As Hawaiians prepared in the 1830s and 1840s to minister to churches in their own land, they began carrying the Gospel to fellow Polynesians in Micronesia and the Marquesas Islands. Sections of this warm-hearted historical volume deal with the adventures of mission workers to the Hawaiian people; to the people of the Carolines, the Marshalls, the Gilberts, and the Marquesas; to the people who came to Hawaii, such as the Chinese, the Portuguese, the Japanese, and the Filipinos; to the "exiles" at Kalaupapa and the Gilbertese in Hawaii; and to "faithful people of all ages, tongues, and races."

Loomis recently published *For Whom Are the Stars?* (Honolulu: University Press of Hawaii, 1976), a documented account of three turbulent years in the history of the country, from the day early in 1893 when Queen Liliuokalani surrendered the throne to the time when her supporters attempted by force to overthrow the republic of Hawaii and restore the monarchy. This period of civil strife is dramatically presented in the first attempt to tell the story with fairness to both sides.

Albertine Loomis, born in 1895, earned a bachelor's degree at the University of Michigan in 1917 (Phi Beta Kappa) and a master's degree at the University of Chicago in 1934. She taught English in Michigan schools before becoming a permanent resident of Hawaii in 1959.

A novel that also covers the early missionary period is *To Raise a Nation* by Mary Salisbury Cooke (Honolulu: Hawaiian Mission Children's Society, 1970). The time of the story extends from 1820 to 1843, when the sovereignty of the Sandwich Islands, after a six-month annexation by Great Britain, was restored to King Kamehameha III. A number of historical figures appear in its pages, but traders MacAfee and Marley, Captain Silas Gulledge, Maka-lolo, and Pualani are fictitious persons. Mary Cooke was a cub reporter on a Kauai newspaper at the age of seventeen and began gathering lore and reminiscences from old-time informants, both Hawaiian and haole. Her book draws not only upon extensive library research but upon consultation with several dozen knowledgeable residents of the islands.

[22] **FRANCIS HALFORD.** *9 Doctors and God.* Illus. Honolulu: University of Hawaii Press, 1954.

The lives of nine medical missionaries to the islands are presented in *9 Doctors and God,* a moving and lively volume by an M.D. from the University of Pennsylvania who spent a quarter of a century in Honolulu and married Marjorie Atherton, a descendant of a missionary family.

When the doctors from America arrived after the long

Medical missionaries journeyed to perilous places to heal the sick, both Hawaiian and haole, according to Francis Halford.

voyage around Cape Horn, these servants of God labored to save lives as well as souls. Their hard-working wives, in a climate quite unlike that of New England, kept households together while their husbands crossed choppy channels by canoe and climbed mountain trails to deliver babies, to fight smallpox and leprosy, and to try to keep alive the Hawaiians who succumbed in thousands to microbes against which they had no immunity. In a day of crude methods, they practiced their craft in the face of opposition from irreligious foreigners, distrustful chiefs, and superstitious natives. The story of the doctors is also the story of a period of great change in the islands, for it covers the critical nineteenth century.

Dr. Thomas Holman, Hawaii's first physician, who arrived with his wife aboard the *Thaddeus* in 1820, is given several opening chapters. The "other eight" are presented in chapters entitled "The Stork and Abraham Blatchely," "Gerrit Judd, King's Counsellor," "Dwight Baldwin, Doctor-Dominie," "Versatile Alonzo Chapin," "Thomas Lafon, Abolitionist," "Naturalist Seth Andrews," "James Smith, Kauka of Koloa," and "C. H. Wetmore, Herbs and Simples." The problems of "the four who stayed" through their lives are dealt with in four final chapters. Seven appendixes offer such valuable facts as notes on non-missionary doctors, a chronology of medical events in Hawaii from 1778 to 1899, a glossary of Hawaiian words, and a selected bibliography.

Francis John Halford was born in 1902 in Cherokee, Iowa, and received his medical degree in 1926. He served his internship at The Queen's Hospital in Honolulu and was one of the founders of the Hawaii Medical Group in 1943. He served as president of the Honolulu County Medical Society and was a member of a number of other medical associations. He received two decorations for working long periods among victims of the Japanese attack on Pearl Harbor in December 1941. Dr. Halford spent fifteen years doing research on *9 Doctors and God,* examining sources not only in Hawaii but in New England and London. The manuscript, which was edited by Thomas Nickerson, was completed just prior to the author's death in 1953.

[23] BRADFORD SMITH. *Yankees in Paradise: The New England Impact on Hawaii.* New York & Philadelphia: Lippincott, 1956.

The most readable account of the mission story from 1820 to 1854 was written by Bradford Smith, a biographer who also published the life stories of William Bradford and Captain John Smith.

Smith, born in 1909, first glimpsed Hawaii in 1931 while traveling to Japan to serve as teacher of English literature at St. Paul's University, Tokyo. During World War II he returned to set up operations for the Office of War Informa-

An entertaining narrative of the Protestant missionary effort from 1820 to 1854 is Bradford Smith's *Yankees in Paradise.*

tion. While collecting material for his volume *Americans from Japan* (Philadelphia: Lippincott, 1948), he became fascinated by the story of the New England missionaries who had brought their modes of religion and education to the islands. After several years of library research, mainly at Harvard, Smith and his wife spent some months in the autumn of 1954 in Honolulu, ransacking the collections in the Archives of Hawaii, the Mission Historical Library, and private collections. Use of diaries and journals was supplemented by visits to sites of old missions, churches, and homes, and by discussions with many scholarly residents. The book contains not only a bibliography and notes on sources of the chapters but a useful list of "Some Important Hawaiians, 1820–1854" and a catalog of "Members of the Sandwich Islands Mission, 1819–1854."

The style of Bradford Smith's book insured that it would be widely read, but his aim was "to find first-hand evidence for every adjective, attitude, movement, and quoted word." He did not omit curious stories of missionary life or aggrandize the achievement of the workers. On the whole, his attitude is one of admiration verging upon awe at the accomplishments of the band of some seventy-five men, and an equal number of women, who set up twenty-two mission stations in all parts of the islands before 1854. Smith's pages cover more than just the mission story; they serve as an entertaining history of the thirty-five-year period he chose to describe in his book, which well deserves a reprinted edition.

[24] WILLIAM ELLIS. *Narrative of a Tour Through Hawaii.* Illus. Boston: Crocker & Brewster, 1825; New York: J. P. Haven, 1825; London: printed for the author by H. Fisher, Son & Jackson, 1826.

Born in London of a poor family, William Ellis (1794–1872) was a gardener before he was ordained in 1815 as a member of the London Missionary Society. He served first in South Africa before being sent, with his wife and infant, to the South Pacific in 1817. Ellis labored for five years in the Socie-

The sport of surfboard riding was described by William Ellis in his *Narrative.*

ty Islands, and was the pioneer printer in the South Seas, with a press set up in 1817.

Captain George Vancouver (see No. 13) had promised King Kamehameha I that he would send him a ship. This vessel, the *Prince Regent,* a seventy-ton schooner built in Australia, sailed from Tahiti in company with the sixty-one-ton sloop *Mermaid.* Ellis traveled to Hawaii on the *Mermaid* in company with the Reverend Daniel Tyerman and George Bennet, members of a deputation from the London headquarters of the Society. The party arrived in Hawaii on March 28, 1822. Before leaving for the Marquesas, Tyerman and Bennet visited the American Congregationalists who had set up a mission barely two years earlier. Ellis remained for a time in Hawaii. His knowledge of the Tahitian language enabled him to learn Hawaiian quickly, and he was the first person to preach a sermon in the latter tongue. He also helped to reduce Hawaiian to a roman alphabet and begin printing in Hawaii. His work was so greatly appreciated that he was invited to work in Hawaii permanently. He agreed, returned to Huahine to bring his family to Hawaii, and entered upon his new labors in 1823.

At that time no mission stations had been opened on the island of Hawaii, largest and most populous of the group. Ellis was a member of a party sent to look for suitable sites for such stations. In June they began a two-month circuit of the Big Island by foot and canoe. The group—which included the Reverend Asa Thurston, the Reverend Artemas Bishop, and Joseph Goodrich—were the first white men to ascend the active volcano of Kilauea.

Ellis's volume is a treasury not only of information about Hawaii during his stay but also of legends and Hawaiian beliefs. His attitude toward them was that of the missionary. "Although he deplored the content of the legends," writes Amos P. Leib in *Hawaiian Legends in English: An Annotated Bibliography* (Honolulu: University of Hawaii Press, 1949), "he was able to find some comfort in the very fact that such legends existed: they showed that the Hawaiians had mental powers which might later be 'employed on subjects more consistent with truth.' "

When Ellis returned to England, he published his *Narrative* in New York in 1825 and in London the following year. It also comprised part four of his celebrated *Polynesian Researches During a Residence of Nearly Eight Years in the Society and Sandwich Islands,* 2 vol. (London: Peter Jackson, late Fisher, Son, & Co., 1829). *Polynesian Researches* was reprinted (Rutland, Vt.: Tuttle, 1969) in a set of two two-volume paperback books. Part four, "Hawaii," consists of an introductory chapter and a brief history of the missionary endeavors in the islands up to 1822. Many interesting and charming passages in the *Narrative,* however, are omitted from *Polynesian Researches.* The separate *Narrative* has been reprinted several times in Honolulu.

In later life, Ellis served as chief foreign secretary of the London Missionary Society and made several visits to the island of Madagascar, about which he issued a two-volume history in 1838. He also published three volumes on the work of the London Missionary Society before his death, when he was nearly eighty, caused by a chill caught in an English railway carriage.

Ellis is an entertaining writer and his accounts of South Sea adventure appeal to readers of his and later times. Robert Southey, in a review of *Polynesian Researches,* remarked: "A more interesting book we have never perused." Ellis's book on Hawaii has been a rich source of borrowings by many later writers.

[25] CHARLES S. STEWART. *Private Journal of a Voyage to the Pacific Ocean.* New York: J. P. Haven, 1828; also *A Residence in the Sandwich Islands.* Boston: Weeks, Jordan, 1839. *Journal of a Residence in the Sandwich Islands* . . . London: H. Fisher, Son & Jackson, 1828.

Charles Samuel Stewart (1795–1870) was an aristocratic, cheerful young man who was trained as a lawyer. A religious awakening aroused him to study theology at Princeton College, and he was sent to Hawaii by the American Board of Commissioners for Foreign Missions. He was accompanied by his wife, Harriet Bradford Tiffany, whom he had married in June 1822, at Albany, New York. The pair lived for two years at the port of Lahaina, Maui, where Stewart and William Richards were the first permanent preachers among twenty thousand Hawaiian residents.

The ship *Thames,* bearing the Stewarts and other missionaries, landed at Honolulu at the end of April 1823. With a sharp eye and keen ear, Stewart began recording his views of native life and customs—especially those of the class of chiefs, with whom the mission was associated closely from the first. Comments range from those on festivals to those on taro cookery. He lists the more important Hawaiians of the period and describes their daily habits and beliefs, of which he did not always approve. Mention is made of haole residents, such as Anthony Allen, a Negro formerly of upstate New York, and Don Francisco de Paula Marín, an exiled

Spaniard. Stewart was acquainted with Kamehameha II (Liholiho) and his queen, and describes the death and funeral ceremonies of the queen mother, Keopuolani, at Lahaina, Maui, where Stewart and Richards set up the first Christian chapel.

The bodies of Liholiho and his queen were returned from London, where they had succumbed to the measles, on the frigate *Blonde,* commanded by George Anson, Lord Bryon, a cousin of the poet. The royal pair were buried in state after an impressive funeral procession and native mourning. Lord Byron planned to spend a month exploring the Hilo region, and the Stewarts, in the hope that the wife's health might be improved, were invited on the expedition. Stewart was among the party that ascended the volcano of Kilauea and made scientific observations there.

The illness of Mrs. Stewart became so severe that the mission members agreed that she and her husband should leave the tropics. Before departing, Stewart made a final visit to Lahaina, where he found that the Richards family were under attack by a gang of forty armed seamen, who were incensed because the missionaries had taught the young Hawaiian women not to break the Seventh Commandment. The intention to kill the family and burn their house was thwarted when several thousand Hawaiian converts rallied to defend their mentors. The Stewarts were able to voyage to London on the ship *Fawn,* and thereafter returned to America, where Stewart was persuaded to publish his journal.

The journal for the years 1823, 1824, and 1825 was originally designed for reading by Stewart's family and friends, but was of interest to people on both sides of the Atlantic. It was edited with an introduction and occasional notes by William Ellis (see No. 24), whom the Stewarts had known in Hawaii and whom they met in London. As the author remarked in his preface: "The original manuscript was written under every disadvantage of place and circumstances; and its highest pretension was that of a true delineation of scenes and characters, as they passed before me; in assuming a printed form, it can prefer no other claim. The only alteration I have made, in a hasty and interrupted revisal of the original, is that of collecting, in some cases, under a single date, remarks and facts upon the same subject found under several; and, in one or two instances only, that of adding, from other memoranda, matters never transmitted to America . . ." Nonetheless, the journal is a highly readable account of customs and events recorded during several critical years of Hawaiian history.

Stewart later became chaplain of the American navy corvette *Vincennes* on a cruise that included Pacific stops at Callao, Peru, and Nuku Hiva in the Marquesas or "Washington" Islands. Stewart's previous stay at Lahaina aided the diplomatic work of his captain when the vessel reached the Hawaiian group. Parties from the ship climbed up to Kilauea Volcano on the Big Island. The *Vincennes* returned to her home port of New York in June 1830. Stewart's book about the cruise is entitled *A Visit to the South Seas, in the U.S. Ship "Vincennes," During the Years 1829 and 1830 . . .* 2 vol. (New York: J. P. Haven, 1831; edited and abridged by William Ellis, London: H. Fisher, Son & Jackson, 1832).

[26] HIRAM PAULDING. *Journal of a Cruise of the United States Schooner "Dolphin" . . . . in Pursuit of the Mutineers of the Whale Ship "Globe."* New York: G. & C. & H. Carvill, 1831; Honolulu: University of Hawaii Press, 1970.

Returning from a voyage to capture any surviving members of the mutinous whaler *Globe,* the *Dolphin* arrived at Honolulu in January 1826, the first American naval vessel to visit the future fiftieth state. Captain "Mad Jack" Percival soon stirred up animosity between seamen in the port and the Hawaiian governing authorities, who were following the advice of Hiram Bingham and other members of the first company of New England missionaries in the islands. An edict refusing to permit Hawaiian women to visit aboard ships in the harbor was the cause of an attack on the home of the "prime minister," Kalanimoku, on Sunday, February 26. On his return to America, Percival faced a court-martial for inciting the riot. He was acquitted because he had also quelled the disturbance after it had started.

First Lieutenant Hiram Paulding, narrator of this lively adventure story, gives only a paragraph to the brush with the authorities—which is covered more extensively by Hiram Bingham (see No. 19). He is a good observer of life in the islands during the four months when the *Dolphin* was refitting, before returning to her base at Valparaiso, Chile. A reprint of Paulding's journal is available, with a lengthy foreword by A. Grove Day.

[27] SAMUEL B. HARRISON. *The White King.* Garden City, N.Y.: Doubleday, 1950.

The White King, about the foremost medical missionary to Hawaii, is virtually a fictionized biography of Dr. Gerrit Parmele Judd (1803–73), who arrived with the third company of missionaries on the *Parthian* in 1828 and spent his entire life in the islands, along with his wife Laura Fish Judd (see No. 28).

The story begins with the decision, in 1827, of young Dr. Judd to seek a change from upstate New York and to sail with the mission group on the five-month voyage around Cape Horn, along with his bride. Through his energy, skill, and judicial mind, Gerrit, although not overly pious, wins the admiration and accord of most of the community, with the exception of land-grabbers and greedy merchants, who burden the Hawaiian chiefs with heavy debts for trifling goods. During the crisis of 1842—when a delegation is abroad seeking guarantees of Hawaiian independence by Great Britain, France, and the United States—the islands are informally annexed by Lord George Paulet, captain of a frigate that threatens to bombard Honolulu unless demands are met. Judd, who has won the confidence of the Hawaiian ruling group, at first serves as a mediator but then breaks with the usurpers, flees to the hills, and secretly sends an agent to London to present the case for the kingdom. The need for an adviser to the throne is so great that Judd leaves the mission, becomes a Hawaiian citizen, and attains several cabinet posts. He is sardonically christened "the white king of Hawaii," but does not abuse his power. The climax of the novel comes in 1853, when a smallpox epidemic gives an excuse for the dismissal of Judd from royal service. He hangs out his shingle as a private medical practitioner and with his devoted wife Laura and eight children founds a family that is still represented in the fiftieth state.

The White King pleasantly interweaves historical and personal events, and characterizes almost all the chief figures in Hawaii in the period between 1828 and 1853, the year previous to the end of the long reign of Kamehameha III. For most of the action, the spotlight is on Judd and his family. The good doctor and his wife are presented as virtually without faults, but it is likely that both were truly admirable characters, and certainly Judd was, even more than Hiram Bingham, the most active member of the New England mission in influencing the history of the Hawaiian Kingdom.

A good historical novel should not markedly violate history, and Harrison seldom is found astray. In the year 1842, when Judd resigned from the mission, however, the population was not three hundred thousand Hawaiians, but about a third of that number. In the novel, leprosy is apparently active in 1828, with a colony existing on Molokai, although historically the disease was not recognized until the 1850s and the leper station on Molokai did not open until 1866. The introduction of the leprosy motif does not seem to advance the plot of the novel. No mention is made in the book of Dr. Judd's guide services in 1840 to the members of the Wilkes expedition that ascended the Kilauea Volcano, perhaps because this episode would divert attention from the political and religious squabbles of the period. On the whole, Harrison committed few of the "small inaccuracies" that are, according to his preface, justifiable in a story. For a standard biography one may turn to *Dr. Judd: Hawaii's Friend,* by the doctor's great-grandson, Dr. G. P. Judd IV (Honolulu: University of Hawaii Press, 1960).

Samuel Harrison was born in New York City, attended Cornell University, and worked in newspaper and advertising offices.

[28] LAURA FISH JUDD. *Honolulu: Sketches of the Life, Social, Political, and Religious, in the Hawaiian Islands from 1828 to 1861.* New York: Anson D. F. Randolph, 1880. 2nd edition, titled *Honolulu Sketches . . . with a Supplementary Sketch of Events to its Present Time (1880).* Honolulu: *Star-Bulletin,* 1928.

Among the third company of missionaries, who reinforced the Hawaii mission when the ship *Parthian* arrived in 1828, were Dr. Gerrit P. Judd and his young bride, Laura Fish Judd (1804–1872). This capable, astute physician, who was to become one of the most powerful men in Hawaii, left the mission in 1842 and held important posts in the government (see No. 27). He was aided by his faithful and observant wife; both of them were destined to spend all their lives in Hawaii. Laura Fish Judd not only served his career but bore him nine children.

Laura Judd's diary—completed in 1861 but not published for almost twenty years—is a mine of information for the social historian and a joy to read if one relishes the views of a New England woman plunged into an active life among Polynesians. She taught a class in an island schoolroom and was a favorite friend of the haughty queen regent, Kaahumanu.

The diary entries reveal dozens of facets of life through three decades: a voyage to another island in a native schooner; the character of Kamehameha III; the founding of Punahou School on land given by Chief Boki; the ascent of Mauna Loa by the Wilkes expedition; the seizure of the islands by Lord George Paulet; the demands of French gunboats; the introduction of plants by Don Francisco de Paula Marín; and the smallpox epidemic of 1853.

"The Old Stone Church" of Kawaiahao, built by the early missionaries, as drawn by Frederick A. Olmsted.

[29] F. A. OLMSTED. *Incidents of a Whaling Voyage . . . .* Illus. New York: D. Appleton, 1841; London, John Neale, 1844.

Francis Allyn Olmsted (1819–1844) was the son of a versatile professor at the University of North Carolina, who was later appointed to teach at Yale. Just graduated from that college, young Olmsted went to sea in search of improved health. He boarded the sailing ship *North America* at New London, Connecticut, in October 1839. The ship hunted whales in the Atlantic and then rounded Cape Horn, heading for the Hawaiian group. Although Olmsted spent only about ten weeks in the islands, in the summer of 1840, he filled six chapters of his manuscript with observations and remarks on the town of Honolulu, surfing exploits, mission life, and the royal family. A chapter is devoted to his excursion to the Big Island and remarks on the bullock hunters who were the predecessors of later paniolos (cowboys), a group of workers still represented by riders on Hawaii's ranches, which include one of the largest under the American flag.

Olmsted returned home on the bark *Flora,* via Tahiti, the South Pacific, and Cape Horn after being away almost a year and a half. Greatly improved in health, he prepared the manuscript of his book. It was illustrated with his own etchings, which were later hailed as the most vivid representations of whaling ever drawn. Olmsted entered Yale as a graduate medical student, but despite a later cruise—this time to the Caribbean—he died in the summer of 1844, just twenty-five years old.

A reprint of Olmsted's entertaining work, with a preface by W. Storrs Lee, was published with the co-operation of the Friends of the Library of Maui (Rutland, Vt.: Tuttle, 1969). Lee stated that Olmsted's account of his stay in the islands is "one of the wittiest pictures of Hawaii created prior to the visit of Mark Twain."

[30] CHARLES WILKES. *Narrative of the United States Exploring Expedition During the Years 1838, 1839, 1840, 1841, 1843*. Illus. Philadelphia: Lea & Blanchard, 1845.

Charles Wilkes (1798–1877), American naval officer and explorer, born in New York, entered the Navy as a midshipman and became an authority on oceanography. While still a lieutenant he was appointed to command the expedition authorized by Congress to make an extensive survey of the Pacific Ocean and the northwest coast of America.

This expedition was the most ambitious scientific undertaking hitherto organized by any nation. It consisted of the flagship *Vincennes* and five other vessels, which set sail in 1838 and spent four years visiting most of the Pacific groups and surveying some 280 islands. Although peaceful in intent, the expedition encountered many adventures, its members surviving shipwrecks and attacks by natives. Part of the squadron also pioneered the mapping of the continent of Antarctica, a section of which is still named Wilkes Land. The most important result of the expedition, however, was the collection of data by outstanding scientists that was pub-

The camp of the Wilkes expedition on stormy Pendulum Peak, during scientific studies on the summit of the volcano of Mauna Loa.

lished in eleven large illustrated volumes. Wilkes himself prepared those on meteorology and hydrography and wrote the official account listed above. This *Narrative,* in which more than half of one volume deals with Hawaii, went through six editions in eight years. The scholarly world became aware, almost for the first time, of the existence of the Hawaiian archipelago as a region of superlative natural wonders and tropical charm.

The ships arrived in Honolulu in the autumn of 1841 and set up an observatory and an office in which to work on charts of the group. A formal call upon the king was well received, and the officers were entertained by the townspeople. However, the arrival of some five hundred seamen with money in their pockets upset the calm of the waterfront, and several sailors experienced life in the local jail.

Teams of scientists explored the island of Oahu, studying fauna and flora, geologic features, and reef and underwater life. In December the *Vincennes* sailed to the Big Island, and the people of Hilo welcomed the newcomers generously, although some missionaries were grieved that many officers did not attend church. The work of the expedition was an important event to the Hawaiians, many of whom assisted in the various undertakings. A procession of no less than five hundred guides and porters accompanied the Wilkes party on the winter ascent of Mauna Loa. There the scientists spent three weeks living in tents and carrying out the most careful survey of the mountain's features attempted until then. Observations on the vibration of the pendulum were made, despite snowstorms and gales, at an elevation of almost fourteen thousand feet. Dr. Gerrit P. Judd (see No. 27), who accompanied the party, had a brush with death on the crater floor of Kilauea. Thereafter a group stopped at Lahaina and ascended the crater of Haleakala, accompanied by students from the mission seminary.

The account by Wilkes does not neglect the social and cultural habits of the Hawaiians; many interesting and informative comments appear on the life of the land in the early 1840s.

A five-volume reprint of the *Narrative* (Upper Saddle River, N.J.: Gregg Press) appeared in 1970. A scholarly and readable study of the expedition, based on many sources, is *The Wilkes Expedition* (Philadelphia: American Philosophical Society, 1968) by David B. Tyler. Two books about Wilkes, who is sometimes called "the American Captain Cook," are *The Hidden Coasts* (New York: William Sloane Associates, 1953) by Daniel M. Henderson and *Stormy Voyager: The Story of Charles Wilkes* (Philadelphia: Lippincott, 1968) by Robert Silverberg.

[31] GEORGE WASHINGTON BATES ["A Häolé"]. *Sandwich Island Notes.* Illus. New York: Harper, 1854.

George Washington Bates spent many months touring the islands in 1853, when it seemed possible that Hawaii would be annexed to the United States. As he wrote in his preface,

FEMALE EQUESTRIAN.

George Washington Bates found that the laws against "furious riding" were not enforced against Hawaiians, such as this "female equestrian."

he tried to portray conditions as they appeared to him in that year. "I have taken special pains to develop the past and present conditions of the people, in their various relations, and have endeavored to specify a few reasons for the 'annexation' of that important group of islands." A final chapter gives reasons for the "necessity" of annexation. However, King Kamehameha III died at the end of 1854 and forty years were to pass before annexation again became a possibility.

Bates drew upon printed materials supplied to him during his visit, but traveled to most of the settled regions of the group and reported his observations in a factual way, interspersed with many poetic quotations. He is an especially good source for details on the agriculture of the period—the growing of sugar cane, indigo, coffee, silkworms, and tobacco, and the rearing of cattle. He calculated, for example, that one square mile of cultivated taro could feed 15,151 Hawaiians for a year. He observed royalty at the "palace," the furious riding of the Hawaiians on Saturday afternoons, the local schools, and the mission stations. His travels took him not only around Oahu but also to Kauai (nine chapters are devoted to this island), to Molokai, to Maui (where he ascended Haleakala), and around the Big Island (where he climbed to the summit of Mauna Kea).

Bates was a proud American expansionist. He was capable of a paean to democracy, and reflected, while boating on the Nawiliwili Stream: "And here, on a Sandwich Island river, were a few American citizens gliding along beneath the ever-glorious beacon of true empire—the 'stars and stripes!' "

[32] O. A. BUSHNELL. *Ka'a'awa: A Novel About Hawaii in the 1850s.* Honolulu: University Press of Hawaii for Friends of the Library of Hawaii, 1972; (paperback) New York: Popular Library, 1973, with title of *The Valley of Love and Delight.*

Oswald A. Bushnell, foremost novelist born in Hawaii, has published three historical volumes that have received wide acclaim.

Ka'a'awa, the first book of original fiction to be published by The University Press of Hawaii, is a novel that opens in 1853, last year of the long reign of Kamehameha III. Hiram Nihoa, minor chief from the valley of Kahana, grew up under the reign of Kamehameha the Great, but adjusted well to the opportunities offered by the incursion of foreigners. Self-styled *niele,* or "inquisitive," he is commanded by the king to spy out the land on the windward shore of Oahu, where a threat of the arrival of filibusters from gold-rich California is rumored. During his picaresque adventures in one or another village, Hiram rescues a beautiful Hawaiian

O. A. Bushnell's novel *Ka'a'awa,* telling of adventures during the reign of Kamehameha III, is based on a lifelong knowledge of Hawaiian culture.

boy who, in the pattern of ancient folk heroes, reveals himself as the last inheritor of the seed of Kalanikupule, king of Oahu.

Hiram leaves the boy with the lad's grandparents in the lovely valley of Ka'a'awa in a hamlet adjoining a ranch managed by Saul Bristol, a self-hating Yankee exile, who becomes the second narrator in the book. Through the influence of spry, extraverted Hiram, Saul slowly returns to life and an appreciation of the happy-go-lucky qualities of the Hawaiian character that make the race both admirable and doomed.

Bushnell's interest in the history of disease in the islands is revealed in the novel, which narrates the effects of the first smallpox epidemic to strike the islands. Much use is made, throughout the story, of old Hawaiian lore and translated chants and songs. The style is pleasantly varied, contrasting the magpie chatter of Hiram with the bitter, introspective journal-writing of Saul. The novel was widely appreciated by mainland readers seeking a historical tale with a setting in the Hawaii of a century past.

Bushnell's earliest novels dealt respectively with the first Europeans to reach the archipelago and with a celebrated experiment in the transmission of the disease of leprosy. *The Return of Lono: A Novel of Captain Cook's Last Voyage* (Boston: Little, Brown, 1956; [paperback] Honolulu: University of Hawaii Press, 1971; English title, *The Last Days of Captain Cook,* London: Chatto & Windus, 1957) covers the period between the arrival of the *Resolution* and *Discovery* at Kealakekua Bay in mid-January 1779 and the departure of the two ships after the tragedy of Cook's death on the shore of that fateful bay (see No. 9). The novel (originally the script of an unperformed play) is narrated by Midshipman John Forrest, an invented character, but also presents many historical persons, both English and Hawaiian, including not only the great Pacific navigator but also William Bligh, John Ledyard, James King, Charles Clerke, James Burney, John Williamson, Kamehameha I, and Chief Kalaniopuu. Several of these characters personify conflicting philosophical attitudes which give thematic point to the various encounters in the plot.

Bushnell's second novel, *Molokai* (Cleveland and New York: World, 1963; [paperback] University Press of Hawaii, 1975), is based not only upon the celebrated service of Father Joseph Damien de Veuster among the lepers of the Kalaupapa Peninsula but also upon a medical experiment. Keanu, a condemned murderer, in 1884 submitted to the transplanting by Dr. Edward Arning of a leprous nodule into his arm in an attempt to transmit the contagion. Arning is the prototype of Bushnell's Dr. Arnold Newman, the cold-hearted German scientist. Other leading characters are Malie, the lovely lady of the court who is exiled to Molokai, along with the brilliant lawyer Caleb Forrest, a Hawaiian descended from the midshipman who arrived with Cook. Newman, Malie, and Caleb each take a turn as narrator of the story, which is filled also with various characters resident on Oahu and Molokai. A sympathetic view of Father Damien is presented as well. Life on the dismal peninsula is recreated with fidelity to fact and medical history.

The story of the publication of *Molokai* is almost unique. One professional reader after another questioned various presumed defects: the narration of the story by three persons; the unusual length of the novel; the discussion of moral aspects; and the possibility that descriptions of lepers might offend the squeamish. One publisher kindly offered to have one of his editors do the cutting. Bushnell finally wrote to his literary agent, in part: "In their preoccupation with Keanu, they don't see that he is the least important of the major characters. In their persistent horror of leprosy, they don't see that the lepers themselves were able to forget this horror and found their happiness in Kalaupapa. And they seem to be so mesmerized by the mere number of my words that they have failed utterly to understand the meaning of them . . . ." Bushnell suggested that his agent burn the manuscript in his winter fireplace, but fortunately, four senior editors at World Publishing Company became enraptured after a careful reading of the novel, and all agreed that it was absolutely right as it stood.

Bushnell, whose grandparents settled in Hawaii around 1880, was born in Honolulu in 1913. He earned a B.S. degree at the University of Hawaii in 1934 and a Ph.D. at the University of Wisconsin in 1937. After teaching at the Georgetown University Medical School in Washington, D.C., he returned to Hawaii as a junior bacteriologist in the territorial department of health. During World War II he served for four years as a laboratory officer in the United States Army Sanitary Corps in Hawaii, Okinawa, and Japan. In 1946 he joined the department of microbiology at the University of Hawaii and retired in 1970 as professor of medical microbiology. His three novels reveal his lifetime interest in the social history and lore of old Hawaii and in the role of whiteman's disease in the extinction of the original Hawaiian race.

[33] ETHEL M. DAMON. *Koamalu*. 2 vol. Illus. Honolulu: privately printed, 1931.

"Koamalu" was the home of a family that for many years after 1854 lived at Lihue, Kauai. The history of that family, their relatives, and their friends is told on the basis of many letters and other documents, aided by recollections of others concerned.

After teaching for some ten years at Punahou School, William Harrison Rice and his wife, Mary Sophia Hyde Rice, went to live on Kauai, where Rice accepted the post of manager of Lihue Plantation. Their four children, all born at Punahou, grew up at Lihue; the eldest son, William Hyde Rice, collected local legends (see No. 5). The eldest daughter in 1861 married Heinrich Paul Friedrich Carl Isenberg, usually called Paul, of a German merchant family. The daughter of this couple, Mary Dorothea Rice Isenberg, married in 1883 a first cousin, the Reverend Hans Isenberg. Thus three families from distant regions were allied and became a part of Hawaiian history. The book ends with the death of Hans Isenberg in 1918, but Lihue Plantation continued to thrive and that story remains still to be written.

The lengthy book contains hundreds of revelations of life on the Garden Island over several generations, and is heavily illustrated by drawings and photographs. The names of dozens of other persons prominent in history appear in the pages, ranging from royalty to faithful retainers. An index and a collection of genealogies make *Koamalu* valuable as a reference work as well as a delight for random reading.

Ethel Moseley Damon (1883–1965) was born in Honolulu and attended Punahou School and Wellesley College, where she earned the bachelor's degree in 1909. She taught at Punahou until 1917, and then served with the American Red Cross in France. Among her other books are several dealing with Hawaiian history and biography. *Father Bond of Kohala* (Honolulu: The Friend, 1927) concerns a missionary who promoted the sugar industry on the Big Island. *The Stone Church at Kawaiahao, 1820–1944* (Honolulu: Star-Bulletin, 1945) is a detailed history of "the Westminster Abbey of Hawaii," which still functions as a Christian church

A painting by Juliette May Fraser of the Lihue Sugar Mill at night, domain of the Rice and Isenberg families of Kauai.

in Honolulu. *Siloama: The Church of the Healing Spring* (Honolulu: Hawaiian Board of Missions, 1948) is the story of a Protestant church on Molokai. *Sanford Ballard Dole and His Hawaii* (Palo Alto, Calif.: Pacific Books, 1957) is a life of the president of the republic of Hawaii and first governor of the territory. *Samuel Chenery Damon* (Honolulu: privately printed, 1966) is the life of the minister who spent forty-two years as head of the Bethel Union Church and Seaman's Chapel and publisher of *The Friend* magazine from 1843 through 1884.

[34] ALFONS L. KORN. *The Victorian Visitors.* Honolulu: University of Hawaii Press, 1958.

A middle-aged English lady with a sharp eye and abundant zest for new scenes and experiences toured the Hawaiian Islands in the summer of 1861. She was Sophia Cracroft (1816–1892), a niece of the renowned Arctic explorer Sir John Franklin and the lifelong companion of his remarkable wife, Lady Jane Franklin. When it was learned definitely in 1859 that Sir John, who had gone in search of the Northwest Passage in 1845, had perished with his men on the northern ice, the two ladies embarked on travels which in time brought them to Honolulu during the reign of young Kamehameha IV and his part-English wife Emma. The charming queen was friendly, and it was her pleasure to entertain these two genteel visitors from her grandfather's country (she was descended from John Young, an English castaway who became one of the most trusted advisers to Kamehameha I).

Miss Cracroft's letters home, supplemented by extracts from the journals of Lady Franklin, give a lively account of the experiences of the two visitors during more than two months in the islands. They not only participated in court life in Honolulu but visited the volcano at Kilauea, relaxed on the Kona Coast of the Big Island, and enjoyed the repose of Hanalei Valley on Kauai.

In a second part, "The Flight of the Chiefs," Korn picks up the narrative when the widowed Queen Emma made a tour of England, France, northern Italy, and southern Germany in 1865 and 1866 and visited Lady Franklin and Miss Cracroft at their London home. A brief epilogue tells what happened to the ladies in their last years. An appendix gives valuable brief biographies of important chiefs, and the book contains voluminous notes to the main entries, which were based on documentary sources from various repositories.

Alfons L. Korn, emeritus professor of English, University of Hawaii, was born in Davenport, Iowa, in 1906 and educated at the University of Oregon; at Oxford University, where he was a Rhodes Scholar; and at the University of California. He became a member of the Department of English at Hawaii in 1944 and retired in 1966. He also collaborated with Mary Kawena Pukui on the collection of poems and chants in *The Echo of Our Song* (see No. 12). Recently he edited and annotated *News from Molokai: Letters between Peter Kaeo and Queen Emma, 1873–1876* (Honolulu: University Press of Hawaii, 1976), an exchange of news a century ago between two native Hawaiians—Kaeo, a leper in the isolation settlement, and his cousin, the dowager queen.

[35] **MARK TWAIN.** *Letters from Hawaii.* Edited and with an introduction by A. Grove Day. New York: Appleton-Century, 1966; (paperback) Honolulu: University Press of Hawaii, 1975.

Samuel Langhorne Clemens (1835–1910), who had only recently begun to use the world-famed pseudonym of "Mark Twain," arrived in Honolulu in March 1866, to spend four months as a roving reporter for the Sacramento *Union.* This first excursion outside his native United States acquainted him with a charming Pacific kingdom. His travels among the islands gave him material for a series of twenty-five sketches written in his inimitable style; one of these was a notable journalistic scoop on a celebrated sea disaster, the burning of the clipper ship *Hornet,* a piece of writing that first made the author a "literary personage." His Hawaii adventures enabled him to embark on a new and lucrative profession—that of popular lecturer. Perhaps the most often quoted remark in Hawaiian literature is Mark Twain's characterization of the future fiftieth state as "the loveliest fleet of islands that lies anchored in any ocean." As late as 1884 he began to write a novel with a Hawaiian setting.

A tireless sightseer, Twain began riding around Oahu in 1866 and reporting his adventures in the capital of the kingdom of Kamehameha V. After a tour of the neighboring island of Maui, where he climbed to the summit of the giant crater of Haleakala and viewed green Iao Valley, he took a schooner to the Kona Coast of Hawaii, rode around the southern end of that island, and scrambled about the Kilauea district, marvelling at the titanic energies of the active volcano. After visiting the sugar plantations of the Hamakua region, he rode along the deep gash of Waipio Valley, crossed the Waimea tableland, and caught the little steamer *Kilauea* at Kawaihae on his return to Honolulu.

The letters, had they been collected soon after their appearance in both the daily and weekly editions of the *Union,* would have constituted Mark Twain's first published book. They cover not only the sugar and whaling industries, which were of interest to American businessmen of the time, but also the Hawaiian trade, whose exports brought high fees to the United States customs service. Much of the material deals with scenery and climate, politics, social conditions, history and legends, Polynesian lore, the monarchy, religious affairs, horse-traders, and even the "millions of cats" of Honolulu. No mention is made of leprosy, brought into the kingdom before 1854, probably because Twain did not wish to frighten off the businessmen who would be his most important readers. The fabulous future of California and the Pacific region is prophesied in letter twenty-three.

A scholarly study of Mark Twain's visit to the islands and later connections is *Mark Twain and Hawaii* by Walter F. Frear (Chicago: privately printed, 1947); it reprints the letters and gives many other items, such as the nostalgic "prose poem."

[36] CHARLES WARREN STODDARD. *South-Sea Idylls.* Boston: James R. Osgood, 1873. *Summer Cruising in the South Seas.* London: Chatto & Windus, 1874.

Charles Warren Stoddard (1843–1909) was born at Rochester, New York, but lived for a time in San Francisco, where he was one of the group of writers that included Bret Harte, Mark Twain, and Ambrose Bierce. He also spent some years traveling in the Pacific, the region from which his best stories, sketches, and poems derive. In 1870, for example, he sailed for the South Seas on a French man-o'-war, and his experiences in the Society Islands produced his best-known

It was "always afternoon" in the sketches and poems of Charles Warren Stoddard.

sketch, "A Prodigal in Tahiti," of which William Dean Howells, who accepted the piece for the *Atlantic Monthly,* wrote some years later, "I think, now, that there are few such delicious bits of literature in the language."

Stoddard, who encouraged Robert Louis Stevenson (see No. 39) to spend his last years in the Pacific, loved Hawaii, and of him Stevenson said: "There are but two writers who have touched the South Seas with genius, both Americans: Melville and Charles Warren Stoddard."

Several items in *South-Sea Idylls* (the British edition is titled *Summer Cruising in the South Seas*) concern Hawaii. Among these are "Joe of Lahaina," about a servant lad on the island of Maui; "The Night-Dancers of Waipio," concerning an adventure on the island of Hawaii among dancers of the forbidden hula; three stories of a Hawaiian boy named Kahele: "The Chapel of the Palms," "Kahele," and "Kahele's Foreordination"; "Love-Life in a Lanai," a sketch; and "The House of the Sun," a description of a ride on muleback into the immense dormant crater of Haleakala, so named because in legend, the demigod Maui is supposed to have snared the sun in his net there.

Other books by Stoddard that deal with the Hawaiian scene are *The Lepers of Molokai* (Notre Dame, Ind.: Ave Maria Press, 1885), dealing with a visit to Kalaupapa; *Hawaiian Life* (Chicago and New York: F. T. Neely, 1894), a series of sketches; and *The Island of Tranquil Delights* (Boston: H. B. Turner, 1904), a further series.

[37] ISABELLA BIRD [BISHOP]. *The Hawaiian Archipelago: Six Months Among the Palm Groves, Coral Reefs, and Volcanoes of the Sandwich Islands.* Illus. London: John Murray, 1875; reprint of 7th ed., (paperback) Rutland, Vt.: Tuttle, 1974.

Isabella Bird (1832–1904), first woman fellow of the Royal Geographical Society, began her travels in her early twenties, in search of health. During half a century, she toured not only the United States and Canada, but also Japan, the Malay Peninsula, Korea, China, India, and the tablelands of Tibet. Already middle-aged when she voyaged to Australia and New Zealand in 1872, she arrived at Honolulu in January 1873, and spent nearly seven months among the islands in this critical year. King Kamehameha V had recently died without naming an heir, and the ill-fated Prince "Bill" Lunalilo was elected to ascend the throne a fortnight before the lady's arrival.

Miss Bird spent little time in Honolulu but sailed to the Big Island, where she enjoyed the town of Hilo, described the Kilauea district during a volcanic outburst, and rode astride to such almost inaccessible valleys as Waipio and Waimanu on the Hamakua Coast. In March she toured the vast crater of Haleakala on Maui, and later spent a month in the serene valleys of Kauai. She was welcomed in the mission stations of Americans as well as in the squalid huts of Hawaiians on wet, lonely trails.

Her book about Hawaii is outstanding even among such other volumes of her writing as *A Lady's Life in the Rocky Mountains* and *Unbeaten Tracks in Japan* (London: John Murray, 1879; 1880). It consists of more than thirty letters written to her sister in far-off Scotland, which have the value of verbal water-colors dashed off on the spot. The tone is inevitably cheerful, even in describing her plight when passing the night in a crowded, grass-roofed shack on a trail where few white women had ever ventured.

The first edition of 1875 was popular, and when a new printing was needed the following year, Miss Bird added some figures to her appendix and otherwise revised the work. A number of other editions and reprints followed. A superb facsimile reprint of the first edition (Honolulu: University of Hawaii Press for Friends of the Library of Hawaii, 1964) not

The volcano of Mauna Kea, "Snowy Mountain," viewed from the town of Hilo. Illustration from Isabella Bird's *The Hawaiian Archipelago.*

only reproduces the original engravings but includes many photographs surviving from the period of the author's travels, and contains a valuable introduction by Alfons L. Korn. The standard biography is *The Life of Isabella Bird* by Anna M. Stoddart (London: John Murray, 1908); a more recent presentation is *A Curious Life for a Lady* by Pat Barr (Garden City, N.Y.: Doubleday, 1970).

Temporary peaks of lava thrown up in Halemaumau during an eruption of Kilauea Crater. Illustration from *Fire-Fountains*.

[38] **CONSTANCE F. GORDON-CUMMING.** *Fire Fountains: The Kingdom of Hawaii, Its Volcanoes and the History of the Missions.* Illus. 2 vol. London: Blackwood, 1883.

A much-traveled English lady wrote a series of chatty letters about her Pacific adventures, giving the feminine view of the islands with verve and precision.

Constance Frederica Gordon-Cumming, of a prominent Scottish clan, accompanied the family of Sir Arthur Hamilton Gordon to Fiji, where this diplomat was the first governor in 1875. A two-year stay resulted in her book *At Home in Fiji* (2 vol., New York: A. C. Armstrong, 1882; London: Blackwood, 1881). She was then invited by the Catholic bishop of Samoa to travel in his company on a French war vessel that showed the flag at Tonga, the Wallis Islands, Samoa, and Tahiti. Her adventures on this trip are told in *A Lady's Cruise in a French Man-of-War* (2 vol., London: Blackwood, 1882).

This author arrived in a sailing ship at San Francisco at Eastertide, 1878, and then headed for the "Sandwich Islands." She made an extensive tour of the group, writing about Honolulu, the North Shore, and other parts of Oahu. She traveled to Hilo, met Father Titus Coan, climbed to Kilauea Volcano, visited sugar plantations, and stopped at Lahaina on her return to Oahu. Her book includes a brief history of the Hawaiian people and the mission effort, and describes the two elected kings, Lunalilo and Kalakaua.

[39] ROBERT LOUIS STEVENSON. *Travels in Hawaii.* Edited and with an introduction by A. Grove Day. Illus. Honolulu: University Press of Hawaii, 1973.

Robert Louis Stevenson (1850–1894), the world-famed Scottish author, first arrived in Hawaii with his family on his chartered yacht *Casco* in 1889 and spent five months exploring the islands, being entertained by hospitable residents of high and low degree, and writing some of his best fiction and essays. Stevenson's step-daughter, Isobel Osbourne Strong, wife of King Kalakaua's court painter, had arrived earlier, and R. L. S. and his wife Fanny were immediately accepted as a part of the royal circle. Stevenson chatted with the half-Scottish, half-Hawaiian Princess Kaiulani beneath her father's banyan tree at Waikiki, and wrote for her a poem treasured by residents and visitors alike.

Stevenson returned to the islands in 1893 for a five-week stay, and found there a changed political climate. Pro-American annexationists had overthrown his friend Queen

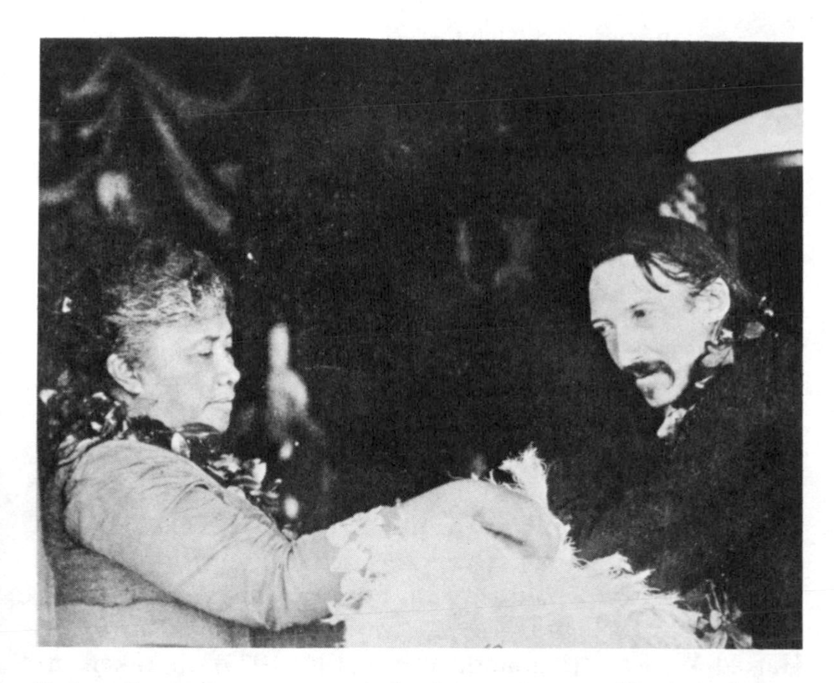

Robert Louis Stevenson and the future Queen Liliuokalani converse at a Waikiki party in 1889.

Liliuokalani and proclaimed the right to set up a republic of Hawaii that eventually was to lead to the establishment of America's fiftieth state. In bad health from an experience with a runaway carriage horse, he nevertheless visited old friends and gave a memorable address to the Scottish Thistle Club. He died on his Samoan estate a year after this final Hawaii visit, during which he wrote little.

His 1889 experience, however, resulted in more literary creation than even the most devoted admirer of R. L. S. might expect. *Travels in Hawaii* includes ten sketches of adventures on the Kona Coast, at the City of Refuge, and on the island of Molokai, where Stevenson spent a week at the guest house of the leper settlement before circling the eastern end of Molokai by steamer and on horseback. Twenty-five letters written from Hawaii by "Louis" and his wife to friends abroad have been preserved, along with half a dozen poems composed to honor Kalakaua and other island celebrities. The volume also contains an appendix transcribing Stevenson's journal of his lone expedition on the Kona Coast, a manuscript never previously published.

Two of Stevenson's best short stories—"The Bottle Imp" and "The Isle of Voices" in *Island Nights' Entertainment*—have settings in Hawaii, and the inspiration for his Pacific novel of adventure, *The Wrecker,* came from an incident reported in the Honolulu newspapers during his residence at Waikiki. The most notorious of his writings about the islands, however, was his attack upon the Reverend Charles M. Hyde of Honolulu, who had written a letter to a California associate defaming Father Joseph Damien de Veuster, Belgian missionary who had died during his labors on Molokai when Stevenson was in Honolulu. This classic piece of searing personal invective, reprinted in *Travels in Hawaii,* is still a *cause célèbre* in Hawaii. For example, much space in a biography of Hyde—*Dr. Hyde and Mr. Stevenson* by Harold W. Kent (Rutland, Vt.: Tuttle, 1973)—is taken up with a full discussion of the charges made in the "Letter," and another view of the dispute is found in a Damien biography, *Holy Man* by Gavan Daws (see No. 10).

The best account of the activities of Stevenson during his two visits is *Stevenson in Hawaii* by Sister Martha Mary McGaw (Honolulu: University of Hawaii Press, 1950). *Travels in Hawaii* is illustrated by a score of photographs surviving from the period of the Stevenson visits.

[40] LYDIA LILIUOKALANI. *Hawaii's Story by Hawaii's Queen.* Illus. Boston: Lothrop, Lee, & Shepard, 1898; Rutland, Vt.: Tuttle, 1964.

The last monarch of the Hawaiian Kingdom, Liliuokalani (1838–1917), wrote her *apologia* in Washington, D.C., in 1897, the year before the annexation of the Hawaiian Islands by the United States. Her biography includes a great deal of island history over six decades, told from the point of view of one of the main actors in the drama.

Liliuokalani, sister of King David Kalakaua and Princess Miriam Likelike, was born in 1838 on Punchbowl hill in Honolulu and reared by Paki and Konia; her foster sister was Bernice Pauahi. Liliuokalani claimed descent from prominent chiefs of the Big Island, such as Kapiolani, who defied Pele at Halemaumau; her great-grandfather, she states, was first cousin to the father of Kamehameha I. She began attending the Royal School at the age of four and later was educated by American missionaries. She married John Owen Dominis in 1862 and went to live at Washington Place, built by his father, a mansion today the residence of the governor of the state of Hawaii.

Her Majesty Queen Liliuokalani, last of the monarchs of Hawaii, whose deposition is described in the book written by herself.

The many chapters of this reminiscence cover her travels around her future domain; her service as heiress-apparent during Kalakaua's trip around the world; her journey as companion to Queen Kapiolani to England via the United States, to attend the Jubilee of Queen Victoria; and the various turmoils that followed the signing of the "Bayonet Constitution" by Kalakaua in 1887. The death of Kalakaua in 1891 resulted in the accession of Liliuokalani; the bloodless revolution of 1893 and the deposition of the queen; the counter-revolution of 1895 and imprisonment of Liliuokalani as a participant; and the presentation in 1897 to the United States of a treaty of annexation that led to the emergence in 1898 of the Territory from the republic of Hawaii. The queen's determination to restore sovereign power to the throne collided with the growing demand for annexation by the United States, the world power closest in geography and in cultural affiliations to the Hawaii of the 1890s. As her opponents said when she demanded the right to proclaim a constitution of her own creation, she had to be taught the lesson "that she is to reign and not to rule."

Understandably, the tone of the book is defensive, but the final chapter—an appeal to the American people to understand the implications of the proposed treaty—is a skillful effort to elicit sympathy for the leader of a Polynesian people apparently subdued by the manipulations of money-hungry foreigners seeking closer business connections with the powerful American disciples of "manifest destiny." The most important place where Liliuokalani's sometimes disingenuous accounts differ from documentary history concerns her attitude when asked, by the new United States minister in December 1893, if she would offer amnesty to the men who had led the overthrow of the monarchy (see chapter forty).

The story of Hawaii by Hawaii's queen ends with her forced abdication and her retirement to Washington Place, where she continued to write songs such as the celebrated "Aloha Oe." She attended the celebration of the opening of the Pearl Harbor Naval Base in 1911, seated with her old enemy and successor Sanford B. Dole. When the United States entered World War I, she flew the Stars and Stripes over Washington Place for the first time, to announce her loyalty in this global conflict.

The volume ends with seven appendixes presenting a newspaper clipping from the San Francisco *Chronicle* (Sept. 5, 1887), statements by the queen, and a series of complicated genealogies of the ruling families.

[41] JACK LONDON. *Stories of Hawaii.* Edited and with an introduction by A. Grove Day. New York: Appleton-Century, 1965.

John Griffith London (1876–1916), adventurer and popular author, sailed his self-designed ketch *Snark* from San Francisco to Honolulu in 1907, and with his wife Charmian spent five months touring the islands before embarking on a two-year cruise of the South Seas.

Jack learned to ride a surfboard at Waikiki, was entertained by Prince Jonah Kuhio and the deposed Queen Liliuokalani, and rode around Oahu. He and Charmian visited Haleakala Ranch on the island of Maui and Jack wrote a graphic chapter in *The Cruise of the "Snark"* (New York: Macmillan, 1911) concerning their trip through the "House of the Sun," the dormant crater of Haleakala. Then they stayed at the celebrated Parker Ranch on the Big Island and watched the bubbling fire pit of Halemaumau at Kilauea Volcano. A visit to the isolation colony on Molokai elicited another chapter about the leper residents there. Jack decided that the horrors of Molokai had been exaggerated, but three of the six stories in *The House of Pride* (New York: Macmillan, 1912) concern leprosy, and his hosts in Hawaii later chastised him in print for dwelling heavily on this aspect of island life.

Two stories in *The House of Pride* are outstanding. "Koolau the Leper," a fictionized version of an actual episode in 1893, gave London a chance to show a strong personality eventually defeated by all the forces of law. "Chun Ah Chun," deriving from his knowledge of the noted Afong family of Honolulu, is a charming story concerning the

Jack London—former sailor, tramp, and gold hunter—made Hawaii his home in 1915 and 1916, shortly before his untimely death in California.

sagacity of a wealthy Oriental paterfamilias of a large brood of marriageable daughters.

Jack and Charmian fell in love with Hawaii and returned there in 1915 and 1916. *On the Makaloa Mat* (New York: Macmillan, 1919), a posthumous collection of Hawaii stories, is on the whole superior to *The House of Pride.* All except the first of the seven pieces were influenced by London's reading of Carl Jung's *Psychology of the Unconscious,* and demonstrate a grasp of mythopoeic power. Had London not burnt out his body at the age of forty, he might have developed into one of the world's most artistic creators of short fiction. As James L. McClintock has written in *White Logic*

(Grand Rapids, Mich.: Wolf House, 1975): "The Jungian stories in *On the Makaloa Mat* are impressive for their dramatic unity, simplicity, and thematic kinship with London's best fictions. They return to London's most productive themes and subjects: death, the conflict between primitive and modern cultures, and the struggle between optimism and pessimism."

[42] CHARMIAN LONDON. *Our Hawaii.* Illus. New York: Macmillan, 1917.

Charmian Kittredge London (1871–1955), Jack's "mate woman" and amanuensis, deserves her own place in the literature of Hawaii. *The Log of the "Snark,"* a voluminous journal published by Macmillan in 1915, intentionally omitted the lengthy commentary on the eighteen-week sojourn in the islands in 1907. This was reserved for her book *Our Hawaii,* which also includes three articles by Jack, "My Hawaiian Aloha," published in *Cosmopolitan* in 1916.

Charmian's *The Book of Jack London* (2 vol., New York: Century, 1921) contains little new on the *Snark* voyage but does add some useful general information, as well as a bibliography. In 1922, after another tour of the islands, she explained in a revised edition of *Our Hawaii:* "This book was originally part of the jottings I kept during a two years' cruise of Jack London and myself in the forty-five-foot ketch *Snark* into the fabulous South Seas, by way of the Hawaiian Islands. The seafaring portion of my notes was published in 1915 as *The Log of the "Snark."* The record of five months spent in the Paradise of the Pacific, Hawaii, I made into another book, *Our Hawaii,* issued in 1917.

"The present volume is a revision of the other, from which I have eliminated the bulk of personal memoirs, by now incorporated into my *Book of Jack London,* a thoroughgoing biography. I have substituted more detail concerning the Territory of Hawaii, and endeavored to bring my subject up to date. Also, instead of making an independent work out of Jack London's three articles, written in 1916, entitled 'My Hawaiian Aloha', I am making them a part of my book, placing them first, because of their peculiar value with regard to vital points of view on Hawaii." The two-volume biography was printed in England (Mills & Boon, 1921); the same publisher issued four two-shilling works by Charmian London, including *Jack London and Hawaii* (1918). *The New Hawaii* (London: Mills & Boon, 1923) contains "My Hawaiian Aloha" and Charmian's section from the revised edition of *Our Hawaii* (pp. 381–427) describing her return in 1919 to the islands after her husband's death. Her last visit was in 1927.

The revised edition of *Our Hawaii* contains 427 pages of writing which, on the whole, is a valuable presentation of island life as seen by an intelligent, adventurous, and articulate visitor at intervals during thirteen years. Her book often sounds too proprietary toward her husband, and the style might repel the male reader; but the frequent descriptions, especially of social events and local hospitality, appeal to women. Charmian devoted herself to perpetuating her husband's memory and achievements.

[43] ARMINE VON TEMPSKI. *Born in Paradise.* New York: Duell, Sloan & Pearce, 1940; New York: Hawthorn, 1970.

A woman writer whose autobiography, *Born in Paradise,* is enjoyed by people of all ages is Armine von Tempski.

Armine's grandfather was a Polish political exile, Major Gustavus Ferdinand von Tempsky *(sic),* musician, painter, and writer, who was killed in the Maori wars in New Zealand. Her father came to Hawaii at the age of eighteen and settled on the island of Maui. Armine was born on the 60,000-acre Haleakala Ranch on that island on April 1, 1899, and literally grew up in the saddle. Her father was manager of the ranch, and the paniolos—cowboys—carried her before them as they rode on their duties. She grew up, with her younger sister Gwen, on the slopes of the titanic crater, "The House of the Sun," and her book tells of wide mountain pastures, volcanoes and tidal waves, viewing a cattle drive when she was only five years old, rodeos and festivals, roping wild cattle, driving herds into the surf and loading them on an offshore steamer, and sharing the life of a ranching family through days bright or somber.

Armine and her sister accompanied the Jack London party (see No. 41) on a pack trip through Haleakala Crater in 1908, and Jack encouraged her girlish efforts to become a writer. Charmian London reviewed Armine's first book, *Hula* (New York: Stokes, 1927), one of half a dozen novels which nowadays are considered much less interesting than the autobiography and its posthumous sequel, *Aloha, My Love to You* (Duell, Sloan & Pearce, 1946). The novels that followed *Hula* are *Dust* (1928), about the desolate island of Kahoolawe, which has been used for many years as a military bombing range; *Fire* (1929); *Lava* (1930); *Hawaiian Harvest* (1935; all published by Stokes, New York); *Ripe Breadfruit* (New York: Dodd, Mead, 1935); and *Thunder in Heaven* (New York: Duell, Sloan & Pearce, 1942).

Armine married Alfred Ball in 1933. She went from her home in Manhattan Beach, California, to Fresno in the winter of 1943 to give a lecture, but stayed in her hotel room because of illness. When her husband did not hear from her, she was discovered in the room several days later, on December 2, dead apparently from peritonitis.

Some details in Armine von Tempski's books were not always appreciated by fellow residents of Hawaii, but nowadays her autobiography, still in print, is warmly recommended by almost every reader.

[44] **GENEVIEVE TAGGARD.** *Origin: Hawaii.* Honolulu: privately printed, 1947.

Genevieve Taggard (1894–1948) is the most consequential American poet to have resided in Hawaii.

Born at Waitsburg, Washington, she was two years old when her parents went to the Hawaiian Islands to teach in the public schools. Up to the time she entered Punahou School in Honolulu, her playmates were almost entirely children of the various races that predominated in the islands at that time—Hawaiian, Chinese, Japanese, and Portuguese—and her writings often show sympathy and friendliness for people of races other than her own. She taught for a year in a rural school near Pearl Harbor and then in 1914 left Hawaii to study at the University of California. After graduation she went east and became an editor, a poet (she published twelve volumes of verse), and a teacher of literature and writing at Mount Holyoke, Bennington, and Sarah Lawrence Colleges. She never returned to the islands, but her recollections of island life appear in such fine stories as "The Plague" (*transition,* Paris, No. 5, 1927) and "Hiawatha in Hawaii" (*Bookman,* July 1929), as well as in her poems.

Five volumes of Taggard poems contain verse about the Hawaiian Islands. A number of these pieces, such as "The Luau," were published in Honolulu by Donald Angus in 1947 under the title of *Origin: Hawaii.* Without being self-consciously exotic, they reveal the color and sparkle of the Hawaiian landscape and the quiet charm of its people.

[45] EARL DERR BIGGERS. *The House Without a Key.* Indianapolis, Ind.: Bobbs-Merrill, 1925.

Best known of the many detective stories with settings in Hawaii (see Appendix B) is *The House Without a Key* by Earl Derr Biggers, which first introduced to readers the suave Chinese policeman Charlie Chan.

The leading character of the book is John Quincy Winterslip, scion of a family of Back Bay, Boston, who comes to Honolulu to persuade his Aunt Minerva to return from her lingering sojourn in the tropics. The murdered man is Minerva's brother Daniel, who had gained his early wealth by shady means in the blackbirding trade. A dozen suspects are examined and dismissed on the basis of clues (such as cigarettes, a brooch, and an illuminated wrist watch) collected by the indefatigable Chan, until the one who could not be suspected is trapped. The Waikiki setting of the early 1920s is used as an integral part of the solution.

In the book, the "house without a key" is the beach residence of Dan Winterslip, where people could come and go in the days when burglary was uncommon. However, the name was attached to a portion of an inn which became part of the Halekulani Hotel. The original section was torn down in 1948 and replaced by a charming cocktail lounge that still functions beneath a spreading monkeypod tree along the beach front.

Charlie Chan is supposed to be modeled on Chang Apana, a celebrated and picturesque member of the Honolulu Police Department, about whose exploits Biggers had heard. Possibly he met Chang when he visited Hawaii in 1919, during which time he gathered material for his novel. The character of Charlie so attracted popular interest that Biggers later made him the detective hero of a series of stories set in various parts of the world: *The Chinese Parrot* (1926), *Behind That Curtain* (1928), *The Black Camel* (1929), *Charlie Chan Carries On* (1930), and *The Keeper of the Keys* (1932). This character was early portrayed in the films by Warner Oland, and the figure of Charlie Chan, with his fractured English and gnomic quotations, is still appearing on television screens.

Earl Derr Biggers (1884–1933) graduated from Harvard in 1907 and worked in newspaper and advertising offices. A 1913 mystery play by him, *Seven Keys to Baldpate,* was widely presented.

[46] MARJORIE SINCLAIR. *Kona.* New York: John Day, 1947.

The best woman novelist of post-war Hawaii is Marjorie Sinclair, for many years a member of the faculty of the University.

Book one (1925–1932) of *Kona* presents Martha Luahine Bell, brought up in the delectable, sleepy region of Kona on the Big Island, who marries Winslow Wendell, a straitlaced member of an ultra-respectable New England family. Marty is the daughter of a Scottish exile who had married a half-Hawaiian girl, and she often enjoys the life of her full-blooded grandmother at her home in Punaluu. But living in

Honolulu, under the rigid rule of her husband and his parents, Marty must suppress the carefree impulses that made her happy in Kona, and slowly she assumes the role of a staid matron.

In the two children of the Wendells, Laurie and the younger Win, the personalities of the parents are embodied. Win is serious and conventional, but Laurie, as revealed in book two (1946), is another "Kona girl," whose inherited drive toward the enjoyment of day-to-day country living is at odds with her family upbringing. It seems that Martha is two persons uneasily inhabiting one body; but Laurie is the fulfillment of the Kona side of her mother's nature.

The incidents of *Kona* subtly contrast the restrictions of city life with the barefoot pleasures of the Kona Coast. "Islanders say that the air in Kona is sweeter and more tender, the sea more fragrant and delicate in hue, the rain gentler and more life-giving. They regard the countryside with a kindling warmth and sigh as they say, 'Kona! There's old Hawaii.' They mean by those words that life is a tranquil enchantment, that the halcyon influence of the Hawaiian people is strongest there."

Sinclair is also author of *The Wild Wind* (New York: John Day, 1950). Lucia Gray comes to Makaniloa, a village on the Maui shore, to see the grave of her great-grandmother, a New England missionary. Lucia soon marries Kaupena Waiolama, a college-bred Hawaiian cowboy, but is repelled by the despair that imbues his failing race with superstition and dark lore. When she goes away with a solitude-seeking artist, she realizes that husband and child are, after all, more important than the yearning for escapist beauty.

Recently, Sinclair published *Nāhi'ena'ena, Sacred Daughter of Hawai'i* (Honolulu: University Press of Hawaii, 1976), the first booklength, fully documented biography of a Hawaiian woman. It deals with the only daughter of Kamehameha I and his highest ranking wife, Keopuolani; Nahi'ena'ena was the ill-fated sister of the future Kamehameha III.

Sinclair is also co-translator (with Lily Winters) of *The Poems of T'ao Ch'ien* (University of Hawaii Press, 1953), from the Chinese and co-translator (with Yukuo Uyehara) of

The Grass Path (Honolulu: University of Hawaii Press, 1955), poems from the Japanese.

Marjorie Putnam Sinclair was born in Sioux Falls, South Dakota, in 1913. She earned a bachelor's degree at Mills College in 1935, winning membership in Phi Beta Kappa, and a master's degree in 1937. She served as registrar of the San Francisco Museum of Art from 1937 to 1939, when she married Gregg M. Sinclair, president of the University of Hawaii. She is a professor of English at the University of Hawaii.

[47] CLIFFORD GESSLER. *Hawaii: Isles of Enchantment.* Illus. New York: Appleton-Century, 1937.

"The aim of this book," as Clifford Gessler wrote, "is to write a national biography and to paint, in broad strokes, a character portrait, illuminated here and there by anecdote, of a country and a people that I have loved." The author's poetic powers and broad understanding of the islands make this more than just another portrayal of their charms for one who might dream of visiting them.

After retelling the highlights of Hawaiian history, Gessler presents scenes of the 1930s: the port of Honolulu, Waikiki, the fishing fleet, sights around Oahu, the military presence, the Big Island, Maui, Kauai, and the cultivation of sugar cane and pineapple. He offers sketches of various types of citizens, and even mentions the early aviators of Hawaii. His descriptions are delightfully enlarged by many good illustrations by E. H. Suydam.

Other books about Hawaii by Gessler include *Tropic Landfall: The Port of Honolulu* (Garden City, N.Y.: Doubleday, Doran, 1942), a fast-paced history of the waterfront, and two volumes of poetry: *Kanaka Moon* (New York: Dodd, Mead, 1929) and *Tropic Earth* (Reno, Nev.: Wagon and Star, 1944).

Born in 1893 in Milton Junction, Wisconsin, Clifford Gessler earned a master's degree at the University of Wisconsin and for a while taught in a high school. He came to

Iolani Palace in Honolulu, as drawn by E. H. Suydam to illustrate *Hawaii: Isles of Enchantment* by Clifford Gessler.

Honolulu as a news reporter, and from 1924 to 1934 was telegraph and literary editor of the Honolulu *Star-Bulletin.* Feeling in need of a change, he joined the Mangarevan Expedition of the Bernice P. Bishop Museum and in 1934 sailed to the Tuamotu group on the ninety-foot sampan *Islander.* His adventures in French Polynesia are detailed in three volumes: *Road My Body Goes* (New York: John Day, 1937; British title, *The Dangerous Islands,* London: M. Joseph, 1937); *The Leaning Wind* (New York and London: Appleton-Century, 1943); and *The Reasonable Life: Some Aspects of Polynesian Life* (New York: John Day, 1950).

[48] WALTER LORD. *Day of Infamy.* New York: Holt, 1957.

On December 7, 1941, at 7:55 A.M. Pacific time, the blow fell on Hawaii that was heard around the world and plunged the United States into World War II. Next day, President Franklin D. Roosevelt opened his speech in the House of Representatives with the words: "Yesterday, December 7, 1941—a date which will live in infamy—the United States of America was suddenly and deliberately attacked . . . ."

A virtually minute-by-minute account of events on Oahu and Niihau is given by Walter Lord, based on interviews with 577 participants as well as reading of voluminous documents and printed sources. The book recreates that eventful day, from before 3:30 A.M. to after 5:30 P.M., especially at the scenes of military and naval destruction. Lord, a skillful interviewer and graphic reporter, makes the hours live again in the memories of hundreds of people who "were there." An appendix gives facts about the Japanese attack and lists the names of 464 eyewitnesses who provided him with written accounts of their activities and thoughts.

Lord, born in Baltimore in 1917, graduated from Princeton in 1939 and served as an editor and advertising writer before publishing *A Night to Remember* (1955), an hour-by-

The Japanese air attack on Pearl Harbor on December 7, 1941, which plunged the United States into World War II, is related by Walter Lord in *Day of Infamy*.

hour account of the sinking of the *Titanic*. Similar volumes followed of eyewitness accounts of other historic events.

Another book about experiences during the "blitz" is *Remember Pearl Harbor!* (New York: Modern Age, 1942) by Blake Clark, who at the time was an instructor of English at the University of Hawaii. Based on many contemporary conversations concerning the impact of the events upon combatants and residents, the volume appeared in February 1942, and soon went through several printings. A most interesting chapter is "The Niihau Story," an account of incidents on the small island of Niihau, where a Japanese pilot crashed and tried to take over the little community; this was the only episode in which the inhabitants of the islands had to deal with an invader.

A personal account of events previous to and including the December 7 attack is *One Sunday Morning* by Ed Sheehan and Robert McCall (Honolulu: Island Heritage, 1971).

[49] JAMES JONES. *From Here to Eternity*. New York: Scribner, 1951.

A best-selling first novel about life in the army (the book is dedicated to "The United States Army") is also the story of a group of people before and during the Japanese air attack on Pearl Harbor in December 1941.

A score of characters are introduced in this big novel, but two army men stand out: Private Robert E. Lee Prewitt, who transfers from a support company to an infantry battalion because he is an independent soul, and First Sergeant Milton Anthony Warden, a career soldier in love with the wife of his captain. Prewitt's talents include a magic skill with a bugle and courage as a fighting welterweight; his recreation includes shacking up with local beauties and a River Street prostitute. The prose of this book shows a lack of skill in standard composition and includes four-letter words shocking at the time of publication, but reveals a raw power deriving from Jones's daily life as an enlisted man in the regular army, stationed at Schofield Barracks, which was attacked from the air on December 7. The volume was a Book-of-the-Month Club choice, won the National Book Award, and was widely reviewed as heralding a new talent in American fiction.

A lesser-known and more unified volume by Jones, also dealing with the Japanese attack and its aftermath, is *The Pistol* (New York: Scribner, 1958). This novella concerns Private Richard Mast, whose sidearm was not recalled after the attack on Schofield Barracks. With visions of being slashed by a Japanese invader with a samurai sword in each hand, Mast clings to this weapon of self-defense in spite of the efforts of his comrades-in-arms to seize it for themselves by force or guile. When he is assigned to guard duty at Makapuu on a windy hillside, his efforts to keep his talisman rise to a peak of vigilance.

James Jones was born in Robinson, Illinois, in 1921. He served in the United States Army from 1939 to 1944 and was decorated with the Purple Heart and the B.S.M. Jones studied at the University of Hawaii in 1942 and New York University in 1945, and worked with Mr. and Mrs. Harry E. Handy of Robinson, Illinois, over a seven-year period. He later published five other novels, written mainly during a residence in Paris, but in 1975 returned to live in the United States.

[50] LAWRENCE H. FUCHS. *Hawaii Pono: A Social History*. New York: Harcourt, Brace & World, 1961.

Hawaii Pono—"Hawaii the Excellent"—stands out as a volume of sociology for three reasons: it concentrates on island life in the twentieth century, under territorial status; it pleasantly avoids the usual sociological jargon; and it is heavily documented.

Fuchs, a student of "ethnic politics," landed in Honolulu in 1957 and began ransacking the library shelves for material on "political acculturation of immigrant groups." He and his four research assistants digested a lengthy bibliography, and fleshed out their notes by five public-opinion surveys and a number of special projects, such as analyses of election returns and campaign attitudes. No less than one hundred and fifty-five "depth interviews" were conducted by the author, who conversed with a wide range of informants, from the former governor Samuel Wilder King to Filipino plantation workers. Wisely, he also drew upon the standard writings of University of Hawaii professors of sociology.

However, the author properly emphasizes that the book is "an *interpretation*—not a definitive history." Rather, it is an account of the coming of successive waves of immigrants, the simmering of a Pacific melting pot, and the struggles of the various Asian groups to win economic and political power. Criticism is disarmed by the author's praise of Hawaii Pono as "the world's best example of dynamic social democracy," but he presents as villains of the drama the "sugar missionaries," annexationists, and Republicans. The earlier Caucasian settlers are pictured again and again as exploiters of cheap, servile labor, although Fuchs does admit that the Japanese workers in the islands, for example, were better off than many labor groups on the United States mainland at the same period.

The style of *Hawaii Pono* at times verges on sarcasm. The group attempting to "Americanize" the Orientals, he says, held a general consensus that Americanization meant "going to Christian churches, playing American sports, and eating apple pie; there was nearly complete accord that it did not mean labor unions, political action, and criticism of the social order in the Islands."

It would be interesting if Fuchs were to return to Hawaii twenty years later and issue a revision of his 1957 researches.

Lawrence Howard Fuchs, born in New York City in 1927, was educated at New York University and earned a Ph.D. at Harvard. At the time of publication of *Hawaii Pono,* he was dean of the faculty at Brandeis University and author of *The Political Behavior of American Jews.*

Appendixes

SOME ADDITIONAL REFERENCES ON THE HAWAIIAN ISLANDS

A. NONFICTION

Adams, Henry. *Letters of Henry Adams, 1858–1891,* ed. W. C. Ford. Boston and New York: Houghton, Mifflin, 1930. Scion of the famed Adams family of New England, historian and traveler, Henry Adams, in company with the painter John La Farge, toured the Pacific in 1890, before writing such classics as *Mont-Saint-Michel and Chartres* and *The Education of Henry Adams.* His letters reveal his reactions to riding around Oahu, sailing to the Big Island, visiting the volcano district, and having an audience with King Kalakaua.

Adler, Jacob. *Claus Spreckels, the Sugar King in Hawaii.* Honolulu: University of Hawaii Press, 1966. A biography of the German promoter from California who for a time dominated the plantation economy of the islands. Professor Adler also edited *The Journal of Prince Alexander Liholiho* (Honolulu: University of Hawaii Press, 1967), the diary kept by the young prince during his travels in 1849–50 to England, France, and the United States. Adler also edited (with Gwynn Barrett) *The Diaries of Walter Murray Gibson, 1886–87* (Honolulu: University Press of Hawaii, 1973), prime minister under Kalakaua and a controversial figure in Hawaiian politics (see chapter 4 of *Rascals in Paradise* by James A. Michener and A. Grove Day, New York: Random House, 1957).

Alexander, Arthur C. *Koloa Plantation, 1835–1935: A History of the Oldest Hawaiian Sugar Plantation.* Illus. Honolulu: Star-Bulletin, 1937. A centennial history of a pioneer sugar plantation, quite readable.

Alexander, Mary C. *William Patterson Alexander in Kentucky, the Marquesas, and Hawaii.* Honolulu: privately printed, 1934. An account of the founder of a prominent missionary clan in the islands. This author has also written another mission biography, *Dr. Baldwin of Lahaina* (Berkeley, Calif.: privately printed, 1953), and, with Charlotte Peabody Dodge, *Punahou, 1841–1941* (Berkeley and Los Angeles: University of California Press, 1941), recording a century of the notable private school in Honolulu.

Alexander, William D. *History of the Later Years of the Hawaiian Monarchy and the Revolution of 1893.* Honolulu: Gazette Co., 1896. An account of the end of the kingdom by a son of the American mission. Alexander also wrote *A Brief History of the Hawaiian*

People (New York: American Book Co., 1891, 1899), an early textbook especially useful for descriptions of pre-Cook civil wars.

ALLEN, GWENFREAD. *Hawaii's War Years, 1941–45.* Honolulu: University of Hawaii Press, 1950. A good narrative history of the home front during World War II, based on documents collected in the Hawaii War Records Depository over a four-year period. An appendix contains a lengthy bibliography and a chronology. A supplementary volume of "notes and references" with "a complete bibliography" was published by the Press in 1952.

ANDERSEN, JOHANNES C. *Myths and Legends of the Polynesians.* Illus. London: Harrap, 1929. Several retellings from the Fornander Collection appear in this volume by a Danish scholar of legends of Polynesia.

ANDERSON, RUFUS. *The Hawaiian Islands: Their Progress and Condition Under Missionary Labors.* Illus. Boston: Gould & Lincoln, 1864. An official of the American Board of Commissioners for Foreign Missions spent four months touring the islands and published his findings at length.

ARAGO, JACQUES. *Narrative of a Voyage Around the World . . . .* Illus. London: Treuttel & Wurtz, 1823, 2 vol. in 1; New York: Da Capo, 1971. Artist on the Freycinet expedition, Arago (1790–1855) wrote an account described by Kuykendall as "somewhat journalistic and cyncial." Letters 104 through 133 deal with the visit to Hawaii. This is a translation from the French of *Promenade autour du monde,* published in Paris in 1822. An untranslated volume by Arago is *Souvenirs d'un aveugle: voyage autour du monde* (Paris: Gayet et Lebrun, 1838, 1840, 4 vol. in 2).

ARMSTRONG, WILLIAM N. *Around the World with a King.* London: Heinemann, 1904. A lively account of Kalakaua's ten-month global tour written by his attorney general, who accompanied him.

BAILEY, PAUL. *Those Kings and Queens of Old Hawaii: A Mele to Their Memory.* Illus. Los Angeles: Westernlore Books, 1975. A narrative of the epoch between the rise of the alii class in old Polynesia and the end of the monarchy in 1893, seen through the eyes of the rulers of the kingdom.

BANDMANN, DANIEL E. *An Actor's Tour or Seventy Thousand Miles With Shakespeare.* 3rd rev. ed., New York: Brentano, 1886. A final chapter of an account of Pacific touring by a theatrical troupe describes Honolulu, visited in 1871 and again in 1883–84. Bandmann met Kamehameha V, Lunalilo, and Kalakaua.

BARBER, JOSEPH, JR. *Hawaii: Restless Rampart.* Indianapolis, Ind.: Bobbs-Merrill, 1941. A short book written in 1940—previous to America's entrance into World War II—in an effort to break the "virtual conspiracy of silence" about many issues that would weaken the feudal hold on the life and economy of the pre-war Territory.

BASSETT, MARNIE. *Realms and Islands: The World Voyage of Rose de Freycinet in the Corvette "Uranie," 1817–1820.* London: Oxford University Press, 1962. Louis Claude Desaulces de Freycinet (1779–1842) commanded an exploring expedition sent out from France in 1817. Dressed in man's clothing, his wife Rose accompanied him on the three-year adventure. This highly readable account includes a description of the visit of the *Uranie* to Hawaii in August 1819.

BAXLEY, HENRY WILLIS, M.D. *What I Saw on the West Coast of North and South America and at the Hawaiian Islands.* New York: D. Appleton, 1865. Dr. Baxley toured the islands in 1862 and wrote several chapters of a chatty, digressive volume concerning his stay. His attitude is not favorable to the missionary endeavors. The best part of his account concerns a three-day trip to Kilauea Volcano.

BISHOP, REV. SERENO E. *Reminiscences of Old Hawaii.* Illus. Honolulu: Gazette, 1916. Born in 1827, Bishop gives accounts, often amusing, of life in the islands between 1820 and 1839.

BLISS, WILLIAM R. *Paradise in the Pacific.* New York: Sheldon, 1873. Bliss, who visited Honolulu in 1872, left an entertaining picture of the city during the reign of Kamehameha V. He remarks on the practices of Hawaiian kahunas or medicine men, the diversions of local society, and the beach at Waikiki.

BLOXAM, ANDREW. *Diary of Andrew Bloxam, the Naturalist of the "Blonde."* Honolulu: Bishop Museum Special Publication No. 10, 1925. A valuable journal by a writer who accompanied Lord Byron to the islands in 1825.

BRADLEY, HAROLD W. *The American Frontier in Hawaii: The Pioneers, 1789–1843.* Palo Alto, Calif.: Stanford University Press, 1942; Gloucester, Mass.: Peter Smith, 1968. Dr. Bradley's well-written and scholarly volume concentrates on the development of Hawaii as a frontier of American expansion. "When, in 1900, the Republic of Hawaii was succeeded by a territorial government modeled upon the precedents established by the Northwest Ordinance of 1787, a century of frontier expansion had reached its logical although long-delayed conclusion." This volume, supported by many notes, brings the story up to the recognition of the independence of the Hawaiian Kingdom in 1843.

BRENNAN, JOSEPH. *Parker Ranch of Hawaii.* New York: John Day, 1974. The saga of a prominent island family and the great ranch that spreads on the island of Hawaii.

BURROWS, EDWIN G. *Hawaiian Americans: An Account of the Mingling of Japanese, Chinese, Polynesian, and American Cultures.* New Haven: Yale University Press, 1947. An ethnic and cultural history of the islands, written from the point of view of an ethnologist.

BYRON, (GEORGE ANSON) LORD. *Voyage of H. M. S. "Blonde" to the Sandwich Islands, 1824–25.* Illus. London: J. Murray, 1826. Lord Byron was commander of the vessel that brought back the bodies of Kamehameha II and his wife from England. The *Blonde* party explored the Hilo and volcano regions of the Big Island in 1825 (see No. 25). The volume was compiled from journals and notes made by gentlemen on the voyage.

CHAR, TIN-YUKE, ed. *The Sandalwood Mountains: Readings and Stories of the Early Chinese in Hawaii.* Honolulu: University Press of Hawaii, 1975. The early history of the Chinese immigrants has been collected in a source book that documents the life of these people from South China on the basis of family histories, public records, and stories of people and their beliefs. A considerable body of writing in Chinese about the Hawaii experience has yet to be translated.

CHEEVER, REV. HENRY T. *Life in the Sandwich Islands* . . . Illus. New York: A. S. Barnes, 1851. A survey of the islands during the last years of Kamehameha III. This missionary visitor favored annexation of Hawaii by the United States. He is also author of *The Island World of the Pacific* . . . (New York: Harper, 1850).

CHINEN, JON. *The Great Mahele.* Honolulu: University of Hawaii Press, 1958. An account of the momentous land-division operation of the latter 1840s.

CLARK, BLAKE. *Hawaii, the 49th State.* Garden City, N.Y.: Doubleday, 1947. A collection of sketches on the Hawaii of the 1940s, with a few amusing excursions into history, by a former instructor in the Department of English at the University of Hawaii. As noted under No. 48, Clark is also author of *Remember Pearl Harbor!* (New York: Modern Age Books, 1942).

CLEVELAND, RICHARD J. *In the Forecastle or Twenty-five Years a Sailor.* New York: Hurst, 1843. As supercargo of the *Lelia Byrd,* which landed the first horses in the islands in 1803, Cleveland met Kamehameha and described conditions on the Big Island at the time.

COAN, TITUS. *Life in Hawaii.* New York: A. D. F. Randolph, 1882. The Reverend Titus Coan served at Hilo from 1835 until his death in 1882. He was one of the foremost evangelists in the revivalist movement of 1837; on one Sabbath in July of that year the Hilo missionaries baptized 1,705 converts and gave communion to 2,400 church members. Three years later, 7,000 people belonged to Coan's flock, making it the largest Protestant congregation in the world at this period. Coan was not only host to many important visitors to Hilo but was the foremost volcanologist of his time, who made many trips to observe eruptions on the Big Island.

COLNETT, JAMES. *Journal of Capt. James Colnett Aboard the "Argonaut" from April 26, 1789, to November 3, 1791,* ed. F. W. Howay. Toronto: Champlain Society, 1940; Westport, Conn.: Greenwood, 1968. Colnett was an early trader and adventurer.

COLUM, PADRAIC. *At the Gateways of the Day.* New Haven: Yale University Press, 1924; *The Bright Islands* (same, 1925); *Legends of Hawaii* (same, 1937). Colum, an Irish storyteller, spent four months in Hawaii in 1923 and wrote three volumes, ostensibly for children, but widely sold in reprint form. The style is influenced by his writing of Irish myths; Genevieve Taggard in a review remarked: "I mistrusted, in spite of the well-known tales from the classics, the peculiar flavor of the Gaelic mind."

CONROY, HILARY. *The Japanese Frontier in Hawaii.* Berkeley: University of California Press, 1953. A well-documented political and economic account of the importation of Japanese laborers.

COOKE, AMOS STARR. *The Chief's Children's School: A Record Compiled from the Diary and Letters of Amos Starr Cooke and Juliette Montague Cooke,* ed. Mary A. Richards. Honolulu: Star-Bulletin, 1937; (paperback) Rutland, Vt.: Tuttle, 1970. An account of the famed school founded in 1839 by missionaries to educate upper-class children. It was dedicated as "the Royal School" in 1846 and put under the Ministry of Public Instruction.

CORNEY, PETER. *Voyages in the Northern Pacific, 1813-1818 . . .* Honolulu: Thos. G. Thrum, 1896. Corney first arrived in Hawaii as mate of the *Columbia* in 1815, and wrote graphic accounts of fur and sandalwood trading and piratical incursions in the days of Kamehameha the Great. An illustrated reprint edition, well edited by Glen Cameron Adams, was published in 1965 by Ye Galleon Press, Fairfield, Wash.

DAMPIER, ROBERT. *To the Sandwich Islands on H. M. S. "Blonde,"* ed. Pauline King Joerger. Honolulu: University Press of Hawaii, 1971. Journal and drawings by the ship's artist of the *Blonde* (see Byron above). This is a beautiful volume published for the Friends of the Library of Hawaii.

DANA, RICHARD HENRY, JR. *Journal,* vol. three, chapter two. Cambridge, Mass., 1968, ed. Robert F. Lucid. After touring Oahu, Dana visited the famed Lono heiau at Kawaihae, Hawaii, made a pilgrimage to the site of the death of Captain Cook, viewed Kilauea Crater, and met D. B. Lyman and Titus Coan at Hilo. There he had a misadventure when a bridge over the Wailuku River collapsed and he plunged with his horse into the water.

DELANO, AMASA. *A Narrative of Voyages and Travels . . .* Boston: E. G. House, 1817; New York, Praeger, 1970. This noted round-the-world sailing master visited Hawaii in 1801 and 1806; chapter 21 of his book describes his later visit.

DIBBLE, SHELDON. *A History and General Views of the Sandwich Islands Mission.* New York: Taylor & Dodd, 1839. Dibble was a teacher of history at Lahainaluna High School (see No. 2). He also wrote *History of the Sandwich Islands* (Lahaina, Maui: Press of the Mission Seminary,1843).

DIXON, GEORGE. *A Voyage Round the World . . .* London: George Goulding, 1789. Dixon's *Queen Charlotte* was the consort vessel of Portlock's *King George.* This book was actually the work of William Beresford, supercargo on the fur-trading voyage.

DOLE, SANFORD B. *Memoirs of the Hawaiian Revolution.* Honolulu: Advertiser Publishing Co., 1936. The leader of the anti-monarchy party recorded his reminiscences of the end of the kingdom. This is a companion to a similar volume of the same title (see below) by Lorrin A. Thurston, the firebrand of the revolution of 1893.

DOYLE, EMMA LYONS, ed. *Makua Laiana: The Story of Lorenzo Lyons.* Honolulu: privately printed, 1945, 1953. Journals of a missionary poet, compiled by his granddaughter.

DRAGE, UNA HUNT. *Hawaii Deluxe.* Honolulu: privately printed, 1952. In 1901 Una Hunt Clarke of Washington, D.C., spent six months in Hawaii. This charming visitor in her early twenties wrote diaries and letters relating her adventures in the society of the time and her excitement in seeing the contrasts in Honolulu at the century's turn.

EMERSON, OLIVER P. *Pioneer Days in Hawaii.* Illus. Garden City, N.Y.: Doubleday, 1928. A life of the Reverend John S. Emerson, by his son. Emerson arrived with the fifth company of missionaries in 1832 and served for many years at Waialua, Oahu.

FARNHAM, THOMAS JEFFERSON. *Travels in the Californias and Scenes in the Pacific Ocean.* New York: Sheldon, 1844. Farnham, a chatty travel writer of mid-century, arrived in Honolulu on Christmas Day, 1839, and helped to popularize the idea of voyaging to Hawaii to see the sights there.

FARRELL, ANDREW, comp. *John Cameron's Odyssey.* London and New York: Macmillan, 1928. The Scottish sea captain John Cameron (1850–1925) had many adventures in the Pacific. He was an officer on the inter-island steamers in the early 1880s and installed machinery at the Mormon plantation at Laie, Oahu. His book is a valuable source for the story of the wreck of the *Wandering Minstrel,* an incident that inspired Robert Louis Stevenson—whom Cameron met—to write *The Wrecker* (see No. 39).

FEHER, JOSEPH. *Hawaii: A Pictorial History.* Honolulu: Bishop Museum Press, 1969. Not just a "picture book," but a well-designed and factual history with innumerable good drawings and photographs from the Bishop Museum collection. Where no good likeness existed, Mr. Feher supplied a sketch. Text is by Dr. O. A. Bushnell (see No. 32) and Edward Joesting.

FERGUSSON, ERNA. *Our Hawaii.* New York: Knopf, 1942. A casual history, with anecdotes of important people and sketches of island life.

FORNANDER, ABRAHAM. *An Account of the Polynesian Race . . .* 3 vol. London: Trübner, 1878–85; Rutland, Vt.: Tuttle, 1969. This giant collection, in Hawaiian and English translation, relies heavily on early oral tradition (see also Thrum, below).

FRANKENSTEIN, ALFRED. *Angels Over the Altar.* Illus. Honolulu: University of Hawaii Press, 1961. A study of charming folk art found in a small church at Honaunau on the island of Hawaii, written by a San Francisco art critic.

FREAR, MARY DILLINGHAM. *Lowell and Abigail: A Realistic Idyll.* New Haven, Conn.: privately printed, 1934. The life story of the Reverend Lowell Smith and his wife Abigail Willis (Tenney) Smith, missionaries in Hawaii from 1833 to 1891, drawn from journals, letters, and other sources by their eldest granddaughter.

FROLICHER, JOHN C., ed. *The Hawaii Book: Story of Our Island Paradise.* Chicago: Ferguson, 1961. A heavily illustrated collection of articles and stories, many of them drawn from issues of *Paradise of the Pacific* magazine.

FURNAS, J. C. *Anatomy of Paradise: Hawaii and the Islands of the South Seas.* Illus. New York: William Sloane, 1948. A somewhat outdated treatment, in magazinist style, debunking the myth of a South Sea paradise.

GALLAGHER, CHARLES F. *Hawaii and Its Gods: The Living Faiths of the Islands.* Illus. New York: Weatherhill/Kapa, 1975. An account, accompanied by many good photographs, of the "manifold houses of God" to be found in the polyracial ambience of the islands.

GAST, ROSS H. *Don Francisco de Paula Marín: a Biography.* With *The Letters and Journal of Francisco de Paula Marín,* ed. Agnes C. Conrad. Honolulu: University Press of Hawaii, for the Hawaiian Historical Society, 1973. Marín, a wandering Spaniard, was a horticulturist, interpreter, and physician for Kamehameha I, and a charming eccentric who kept a diary and corresponded with many persons around the Pacific.

GEROULD, KATHERINE FULLERTON. *Hawaii: Scenes and Impressions.* New York: Scribner, 1916. A well-known essayist gives her views of scenes in the islands before World War I.

GOODHUE, EDWARD S. *Beneath Hawaiian Palms and Stars.* Cincinnati, O.: Editor Pubishing Co., 1900. Physician, scientist, and businessman, Dr. Goodhue visited the islands in 1898, year of annexation, and wrote three books giving his views of America's new territory. The treatment is somewhat flippant, but Clarice Taylor recommended it as "a forgotten treasure."

GOWEN, HERBERT H. *The Napoleon of the Pacific: Kamehameha the Great.* New York: Revell, 1919. An early biography of Kamehameha that emphasizes his skill in attracting foreign advisers and artisans to his cause.

GRAY, FRANCINE. *Hawaii: The Sugar-Coated Fortress.* New York: Random House, 1972. An opinionated, ultra-liberal view of contemporary Hawaii by a visitor, based mainly on interviews.

GUGLIOTTA, BOBETTE. *Nolle Smith: Cowboy, Engineer, Statesman.* Illus. New York: Dodd, Mead, 1971. Nolle Smith, son of a Scottish-Irish Wyoming rancher and his Negro-Indian wife, came to Hawaii as a public-works engineer and rose to be a member of the Legislature and Director of Civil Service. Later he served the U.S. State Department in Ecuador, Haiti, and Brazil.

GULICK, REV. and MRS. O. H. *The Pilgrims of Hawaii.* New York: Fleming H. Revell, 1918. A history of the Protestant mission taken mainly from diaries and journals.

HAAR, FRANCIS and NEOGY, PRITHWISH. *Artists of Hawaii: Nineteen Painters and Sculptors.* Honolulu: University Press of Hawaii, 1974. A variety of contemporary artists residing in the state reveal a number of styles and attitudes at work.

HARDY, THORNTON S. *Wallace Rider Farrington.* Illus. Honolulu: Star-Bulletin, 1935. Biography of one of Hawaii's governors.

HOPKINS, MANLEY. *Hawaii: The Past, Present, and Future of Its Island-Kingdom* . . . . London: Longman, Green, Longman & Roberts, 1862; rev. ed. 1866. Hopkins (1818–1897) served as consul-general for Hawaii in England for more than forty years. He never visited the islands but his brother, Charles Gordon Hopkins, was in the Hawaiian government for some years and furnished much material. This early history was written partly to acquaint the British public with the need for establishing the Anglican church in Hawaii. Manley Hopkins was the father of the English poet Gerard Manley Hopkins.

HOBBS, JEAN FORTUNE. *Hawaii: A Pageant of the Soil.* Palo Alto, Calif.: Stanford University Press, 1935. A history of land ownership in the islands.

HUNNEWELL, JAMES F. *Journal of the Voyage of the "Missionary*

Packet," Boston to Honolulu, 1826. Charlestown, Mass.: privately printed, 1880. Hunnewell was a pioneer merchant in Honolulu who made several round-the-Horn voyages under dangerous conditions.

INGRAHAM, JOSEPH. *Journal of the Brigantine "Hope" . . . ,* ed. M. Kaplanoff. Barre, Mass.: Imprint Society, 1971. Ingraham first saw the islands as second mate of the *Columbia* in 1789, and returned twice in 1791 as master of the *Hope.* This brigantine barely escaped being captured by Kamehameha I, a fate that befell the schooner *Fair American.* The journal is quite readable, since Ingraham's work was "intended for landsmen to amuse themselves with."

INOUYE, DANIEL K. and ELLIOTT, LAWRENCE. *Journey to Washington.* Englewood Cliffs, N.J.: Prentice-Hall, 1967. Autobiography of the veteran of the 442nd Division during World War II who became the first United States senator of Japanese descent.

JACKS, LEO V. *Mother Marianne of Molokai.* New York: Macmillan, 1935. Mother Marianne led the first group of the Sisters of St. Francis to Molokai to continue the work of Father Damien and to establish a home for girls at the colony.

JOHANNESSEN, EDWARD. *The Hawaiian Labor Movement.* Illus. Boston: Bruce Humphries, 1956. A history of the development of union labor in the islands.

JUDD, LAWRENCE M. *Lawrence M. Judd and Hawaii: An Autobiography,* as told to Hugh W. Lytle. Rutland, Vt.: Tuttle, 1971. A grandson of Dr. G. P. Judd (see No. 27) narrates events in the life of an active descendant who served as the seventh governor of the Territory of Hawaii and governor of American Samoa.

KALAKAUA, DAVID. *The Legends and Myths of Hawaii.* New York: C. L. Webster, 1888. "Edited and with an introduction by Hon. R. M. Daggett, Late United States Minister to the Hawaiian Islands." Political and historical traditions of the pre-Cook period make up most of this collection. Amos P. Leib says that "whether Kalakaua's contribution to the book was great enough to enable him to be called its author, except through the courtesy of Daggett, is doubtful . . . . Daggett was probably the author."

KENT, HAROLD W. *Charles Reed Bishop, Man of Hawaii.* Palo Alto, Calif.: Pacific Books, 1965. The life and times of a New Yorker who became a leading businessman and government official in Honolulu, and married Bernice Pauahi, heiress of the Kamehameha line. The wife's fortune became the Bishop Estate, income from which supports The Kamehameha Schools, and Bishop's own estate went to the support of the Bernice P. Bishop Museum. Kent is also author of *Dr. Hyde and Mr. Stevenson: The Life of the Rev. Dr. Charles McEwen Hyde* (see No. 39).

KNUDSEN, E. A. and NOBLE, GURRE P. *Kanuka of Kauai.* Honolulu: Tongg Publishing Co., 1944. The life of Valdemar Knudsen, son of a premier of Norway, who lost the gold he acquired in the California rush but made a new fortune in sugar on the island of Kauai.

KRAUSS, BOB, with W. P. ALEXANDER. *Grove Farm Plantation.* Palo Alto, Calif.: Pacific Books, 1965. The story of a Kauai sugar plantation and of George N. Wilcox, the man who developed an important property and became a power in Hawaiian politics. Krauss, a Honolulu journalist, also wrote collections of essays: *Here's Hawaii* and *High-Rise Hawaii* (New York: Coward-McCann, 1960, 1964).

KROUT, MARY H. *Hawaii and a Revolution.* New York: Dodd, Mead, 1898. Appearing during the year of annexation, this account of the revolution of 1893 and the deposition of Queen Liliuokalani was based on a visit in 1893 by this Chicago journalist. Her sources all favored annexation. Miss Krout is also author of *The Memoirs of the Honorable Bernice Pauahi Bishop* (New York: Knickerbocker Press, 1908), heiress of the Kamehameha dynasty.

KRUSENSTERN, ADAM JOHANN VON. *A Voyage Round the World* (London: printed by C. Roworth for J. Murray, 1813), trans. R. B. Hoppner from the German edition. Krusenstern's ship *Nadeshda,* on a round-the-world voyage for the Russian Imperial Navy, was accompanied by the *Neva,* whose captain, Urey Lisiansky, translated his own account into English in *A Voyage Round the World* (London: printed for J. Booth, 1814). Both ships visited Hawaii in 1804.

LA FARGE, JOHN. *Reminiscences of the South Seas.* Illus. New York: Doubleday, Page, 1912. La Farge, painter and writer, in 1890–91 traveled in company with Henry Adams to various parts of the Pacific, including Hawaii.

LEMON, SISTER ADELE MARIE. *Hawaii, Lei of Islands: A History of Catholic Hawaii.* Illus. Honolulu: Tongg, 1956. The story is told from the Catholic point of view, with lives of the Catholic missionaries, simply written.

LIND, ANDREW W. *Hawaii's People.* Honolulu: University of Hawaii Press, 1967. A straightfoward account of the origins of the polyracial population, their status today, and the biological fusions being formed for the future, by an emeritus professor of sociology at the University of Hawaii. Lind is also author of *An Island Community: Ecological Succession in Hawaii* (Chicago: University of Chicago Press, 1938) and *Hawaii's Japanese: An Experiment in Democracy* (Princeton, N.J.: Princeton University Press, 1946).

LING-AI, LI. *Life Is for a Long Time.* New York: Hastings House, 1973. Lives and beliefs of a husband-and-wife medical team that migrated from China to Hawaii at the turn of the century.

LYMAN, CHESTER S. *Around the Horn to the Sandwich Islands and California, 1845–1850.* New Haven: Yale University Press, 1924. Lyman gives some fine vignettes of adventure in the islands, such as surfing at Waikiki with royal children, Titus Coan's preaching during the "Great Awakening," a trip to Kilauea, and Hawaiian "Thugs."

LYMAN, HENRY M. *Hawaiian Yesterdays: Chapters from a Boy's Life in Hawaii in the Islands in the Early Days.* Chicago: A. C. McClurg, 1906. Recollections of a missionary son (1835–1904) who spent most of his life in Hilo as a physician, educator, and writer.

MACDONALD, ALEXANDER. *Revolt in Paradise.* New York: Stephen Daye, 1944. An account of "the social revolution in Hawaii after Pearl

Harbor," published during World War II to show that "a new order is being established in Hawaii."

MENZIES, ARCHIBALD. *Hawaii Nei 128 Years Ago,* ed. W. F. Wilson. Honolulu: New Freedom Press, 1920. Menzies, an accomplished naturalist, visited Hawaii in 1787–88 on the *Prince of Wales* and on Vancouver's *Discovery* in 1792–94. In 1794 he ascended the summit of Mount Hualalai and, with the aid of Kamehameha I, led a party up the slope of Mauna Loa over a trail still bearing his name.

MORGAN, THEODORE. *Hawaii: A Century of Economic Change, 1778–1876.* Cambridge, Mass.: Harvard University Press, 1948. A scholarly study of the earlier post-Cook period, covering the fur and sandalwood trades, whaling, and the rise of the sugar business. A solid economic history of the Hawaiian Islands still remains to be written.

MOURITZ, ARTHUR ALBERT ST. M. *The Path of the Destroyer: A History of Leprosy in the Hawaiian Islands.* Honolulu: Star-Bulletin, 1916. A rare and valuable account by a French medical doctor of the growth of the disease in the islands.

MULHOLLAND, JOHN F. *Hawaii's Religions.* Rutland, Vt.: Tuttle, 1970. Chronologies of the various religions found in the islands from ancient times to the present.

MURPHY, THOMAS D. *Ambassadors in Arms.* Honolulu: University of Hawaii Press, 1954. When the Pearl Harbor attack plunged the United States into World War II, the Japanese people of Hawaii were anxious to show their loyalty. Thousands of young "Americans of Japanese Ancestry" volunteered to serve in the armed forces. This history of the 100th Infantry Battalion (later part of the 442nd Regimental Combat Team) as told by Professor Murphy is one of the most moving accounts of modern warfare. The battalion landed at Salerno in September 1943, and fought so valiantly in the Italian and French campaigns that by V-E Day they were designated by experts as "probably the most decorated unit in the United States military history." Other AJA's served in Pacific engagements from Guadalcanal to Okinawa.

NICOL, JOHN. *The Life and Adventures of John Nicol, Mariner . . .* Edinburgh: William Blackwood; London: T. Cadell, 1822; New York: Farrar & Rinehart, 1936. Nicol was cooper on the *King George,* Nathaniel Portlock's flagship, which visited Hawaii several times in 1786–88. Alexander Laing, editor of the illustrated 1936 edition, calls this work "prose surpassed in its kind by none but that of Melville."

NORDHOFF, CHARLES. *Northern California, Oregon, and the Sandwich Islands.* New York: Harper, 1874. Bluejacket in the United States Navy, newspaper editor and correspondent, travel writer, Nordhoff visited Hawaii in 1873 and toured Oahu, Kauai, and the Big Island. This author was the grandfather of Charles Nordhoff, collaborator with James Norman Hall.

NOTTAGE, CHARLES G. *In Search of a Climate.* Illus. London: S. Low, Marston, 1894. An English Fellow of the Royal Geographical Society devotes five chapters of a chatty travel book to "the Sandwich

Islands,'' reporting on a visit to Kilauea, the activities of missionary descendants, and the revolution of 1893.

OLIVER, DOUGLAS. *The Pacific Islands.* Cambridge: Harvard University Press, 1951; 1961; rev. ed., (paperback) Honolulu: University Press of Hawaii, 1975. Hawaii in the perspective of the development of Oceania during the two centuries past.

PARKE, WILLIAM C. *Personal Reminiscences.* Cambridge, Mass.: Harvard University Press, 1891. Recollections of the marshal of the kingdom from 1850 to 1884, arranged by his son.

PERKINS, EDWARD T. *Na Motu; or, Reef-Rovings in the South Seas.* Illus. New York: Pudney & Russell, 1854. Perkins sailed to Hawaii in 1848 and spent twenty months in the group before leaving for the Society Islands. In a confidential style he reveals many aspects of life, grave and gay. An appendix gives useful information on Polynesia, Hawaii, the French in the Pacific, and the American whaling interests in that ocean.

PIERCE, RICHARD A. *Russia's Hawaiian Adventure, 1815–1817.* Berkeley, Calif.: University of California Press, 1965. A narrative based on documents concerning the Russian attempt to take over the islands.

PORTEUS, STANLEY D. *Calabashes and Kings: An Introduction to Hawaii.* Palo Alto, Calif.: Pacific Books, 1954; Rutland, Vt.: Tuttle, 1970. A discursive and semi-humorous series of sketches by a long-time resident and professor of psychology. Porteus also wrote *And Blow Not the Trumpet* (Palo Alto, Calif.: Pacific Books, 1947), an account of the contributions of the sugar industry in World War II, and edited *A Century of Social Thinking in Hawaii* (same, 1962), a collection of essays presented before the Social Science Association of Honolulu by various members over a period of eighty-two years (see also No. 14).

PORTLOCK, NATHANIEL. *A Voyage Round the World . . . in the "King George" and "Queen Charlotte."* London: John Stockdale & George Goulding, 1789. Portlock led a fur-hunting expedition to the Northwest Coast, which spent the winters of 1786–88 in Hawaii. His account gives an excellent story of the first adventurers in Hawaii after the death of Cook.

PRATT, HELEN GAY. *Hawaii: Off-Shore Territory.* New York: Scribner, 1944. An elementary history of the islands from 1898 to 1941.

PRATT, JOHN SCOTT BOYD, JR. *The Hawaii I Remember.* Illus. Kaneohe, Hawaii: privately printed, 1965. A great-grandson of Dr. Gerrit P. Judd (see No. 27) and a member of a prominent Honolulu family recalls the life of the city seventy years ago.

PRATT, JULIUS W. *Expansionists of 1898: The Acquisition of Hawaii and the Spanish Islands.* Baltimore: Johns Hopkins Press, 1936; New York: Peter Smith, 1951. A scholarly study of annexation as an example of America's "manifest destiny."

RESTARICK, BISHOP H. B. *Hawaii, 1778–1920, from the Viewpoint of a Bishop.* Honolulu: Paradise of the Pacific, 1924, 1925. A history of the Anglican and Episcopal church in Hawaii.

REYNOLDS, STEPHEN. *Voyage of the "New Hazard," 1810–1813,* ed.

F. W. Howay. Salem, Mass.: Peabody Museum, 1938. Reynolds made three visits to Hawaii on this ship in 1811 and 1812. During a fourth visit this American seaman arrived on the *Isabella* and returned on the *New Hazard*. In 1822 he returned to reside in Honolulu as merchant, lawyer, and harbor master.

RUSCHENBERGER, WILLIAM S. *A Voyage Round the World, 1835–37.* Philadelphia: Carey, Lea & Blanchard, 1838. The fleet surgeon of the round-the-world voyage of the U.S.S. *Peacock* visited the "Sandwich Islands" in 1836. Fifty pages are devoted to sketches of the court, the missionaries, and the Hawaiian people. Commodore E. P. Kennedy discussed various American claims with the rulers in diplomatic fashion.

RUSS, WILLIAM A. *The Hawaiian Revolution. 1893–94.* Selinsgrove, Penna.: Susquehanna University Press, 1959. A scholarly study of the revolution and the American interest in the islands. Russ is also author of a sequel, *The Hawaiian Republic, 1894–1898, and the Struggle to Win Annexation* (same, 1961).

SIMPICH, FREDERICK, JR. *Anatomy of Hawaii.* New York: Coward, McCann & Geoghegan, 1971. Description of the business scene in 1970 by a long-time observer, containing some minor inaccuracies.

SIMPSON, SIR GEORGE. *Narrative of a Journey Round the World, During the Years 1841 and 1842.* Philadelphia: Lea & Blanchard, 1847; London: H. Colburn, 1847. Governor of the Hudson's Bay Company, Sir George understood the need for international recognition of the independence of the kingdom.

STEEGMULLER, FRANCIS. *The Two Lives of James Jackson Jarves.* New Haven, Conn.: Yale University Press, 1951. A scholarly study of the achievements of Jarves (see No. 7) in Hawaii and Europe.

STEVENS, SYLVESTER K. *American Expansion in Hawaii, 1842–1898.* Harrisburg, Penna.: Archives Publishing Co., 1945; New York: Russell & Russell, 1968. A scholarly study of early relations that might be considered a sequel to that by Harold W. Bradley (see above).

TAYLOR, ALBERT P. *Under Hawaiian Skies.* Honolulu: Advertiser, 1922, 1926. A discursive and anecdotal history by a newspaper man and archivist of the Territory of Hawaii.

TAYLOR, FITCH W. *The Flag Ship: or a Voyage Around the World, in the United States Frigate "Columbia."* 2 vol. Illus. New York: D. Appleton, 1840. The chaplain of the squadron led by the *Columbia* on a round-the-world voyage visited Hawaii in 1839. Section eight describes the reception of the ship's officers in Honolulu and their support of the efforts of the American missionaries in the islands.

TAYLOR, FRANK J., WELTY, EARL M., and EYRE, DAVID W. *From Land and Sea: The Story of Castle & Cooke of Hawaii.* San Francisco: Chronicle Books, 1976. An outstanding, well-illustrated corporate history, covering the period from the arrival of the missionary founders in 1837 up until 1975, when this member of the "Big Five" was a multinational leader. Appendixes and bibliography.

THRUM, THOMAS G. *Hawaiian Folk Tales: a Collection of Native Legends.* Chicago: A. C. McClurg, 1907. Thrum published this and several other volumes of selections of legends that had appeared in his

Hawaiian Almanac and Annual, which began publication in 1875. He also edited and translated *The Fornander Collection of Hawaiian Antiquities and Folklore,* Honolulu: Bishop Museum, *Memoirs,* V, 1916–1920, deriving from various sources; it is the greatest single repository of Hawaiian folklore.

THURSTON, LORRIN ANDREWS. *Memoirs of the Hawaiian Revolution.* Illus. Honolulu: Advertiser, 1936. Originally a series of articles in the *Advertiser* newspaper, the chapters cover early recollections as well as the revolution.

TYERMAN, DANIEL and BENNET, GEORGE. *Journal of Voyages and Travels . . . compiled from original documents by James Montgomery.* 2 vol. Boston: Crocker & Brewster; London: F. Westley & A. H. Davis, 1831. Tyerman and Bennet, a deputation of the London Missionary Society to the Pacific, arrived in Hawaii in March 1822, in company with William Ellis (see No. 24), and their report is based heavily upon his *Polynesian Researches.*

VAN SLINGERLAND, PETER. *Something Terrible Has Happened.* New York: Harper, 1966. One of several journalistic reviews of the notorious Massey murder case of 1931 and its effect upon the political situation in the islands.

VANDERCOOK, J. W. *King Cane: The Story of Sugar in Hawaii.* New York: Harper, 1939. A readable but somewhat superficial and outdated story of the development of the sugar industry.

WALDRON, ELSE SCHAEFER. *Honolulu a Hundred Years Ago.* Illus. Honolulu: Fisher, 1967. Local diaries, anecdotes, and letters, especially concerning the Judge Robertson and Schaefer families.

WARRINER, EMILY V. *Voyager to Destiny.* Illus. Indianapolis, Ind.; Bobbs-Merrill, 1956. The amazing life of Nakahama Manjiro, who as a youth was rescued from a wrecked fishing vessel and taken to Honolulu. From there he went to Fairhaven, Massachusetts, and was given an American education; he was, actually, the first Japanese to come to the United States and to be educated there. He later rose to leadership in Japanese diplomacy and naval affairs.

WARRINER, FRANCIS. *Cruise of the United States Frigate "Potomac" . . . .* Illus. New York: Leavitt, Lord, 1835. An officer aboard the *Potomac* on a round-the-world voyage to show the flag during 1831–34 devotes chapter 19 to a visit to Honolulu and discussions with King Kamehameha III and his advisers.

WEBB, NANCY and JEAN. *Kaiulani: Crown Princess of Hawaii.* New York: Viking, 1962. Life story of Hawaii's charming heiress-apparent.

WESTERVELT, WILLIAM D. *Legends of Ma-ui . . . .* Honolulu: Gazette, 1910. Westervelt was a popularizer who collected and interpreted legends from various sources. From his many articles he published four books; in addition to the Maui volume, these are *Legends of Old Honolulu* (1915), *Legends of Gods and Ghosts* (1915), and *Hawaiian Legends of Volcanoes* (1916; all published by Ellis Press, Boston). The last three are available in reprint form (Rutland, Vt.: Tuttle, 1973).

WISE, HENRY A. *Los Gringos: or An Inside View of . . . Polynesia.* New York: Baker & Scribner, 1849; London: R. Bentley, 1849. A lieutenant in the American Navy made a Pacific cruise in 1846–47 and spent forty days at Hilo, Lahaina, and Honolulu, where the officers were presented at the court of Kamehameha III. Chapters 39 through 44 deal with Hawaii. The object of the author was "merely to compile a pleasant narrative."

WIST, BENJAMIN C. *A Century of Public Education in Hawaii, October 15, 1840 to October 15, 1940.* Honolulu: Hawaii Educational Review, 1940. The best available history of the development of education in the islands, by a former dean of the School of Education, University of Hawaii.

WITHINGTON, ANTOINETTE, *Hawaiian Tapestry.* Illus. New York: Harper, 1937. Charming sketches of life in the islands previous to World War II. Mrs. Withington is also author of *The Golden Cloak* (Honolulu: Hawaiian Press, 1953, illus.), an informal and detailed history of Hawaiian notables to 1893.

WRIGHT, THEON. *The Disenchanted Isles: The Story of the Second Revolution in Hawaii.* New York: Dial, 1972. Journalistic account of the contemporary scene.

WRIGHT, LOUIS B. and FRY, MARY ISABEL. *Puritans in the South Seas.* New York: Henry Holt, 1936. Two collaborators from the Huntington Library, San Marino, California, wrote a highly readable account of Protestant missionaries in the Pacific. Chapter eleven, "Boston Puritans in the Promised Land," deals amusingly with the early mission to Hawaii.

YOST, HAROLD, H. *The Outrigger: A History of the Outrigger Canoe Club, 1908–1917.* Illus. Honolulu: privately printed, 1971. More than the title implies, this beautifully illustrated story of the growth of the famous Waikiki beach facility also includes many sketches of twentieth-century scenes in Honolulu since 1908. Yost is also author (with Alex Castro) of *The Hawaii Almost Nobody Remembers* (Honolulu: privately printed, 1972), a collection of short essays.

YOUNG, LUCIEN. *The "Boston" at Hawaii . . .* Washington, D.C.: Gibson, 1898. The author came to the islands in 1892 on an American man-o'-war that stayed for fourteen months. The book, which describes the reign of Liliuokalani and the establishment of the republic, was expanded and published as *The Real Hawaii* (New York: Doubleday, 1899).

YZENDOORN, REGINALD. *History of the Catholic Mission in the Hawaiian Islands.* Honolulu: Star-Bulletin, 1927. A detailed account, especially good for the early years of the Catholic mission.

B. FICTION

BASSETT, JAMES. *Harm's Way.* New York: World, 1962. This novel of naval adventures in World War II opens on December 7, 1941, and during the succeeding months follows the career of Rear Admiral Rockwell Torrey, charged with a dangerous mission in command of an outmoded task force in the Pacific. A paperback Signet reprint was retitled *In Harm's Way.*

BRANCH, HOUSTON, and WATERS, FRANK. *Diamond Head.* New York:

Farrar, Straus, 1948. A novel about the notorious Confederate raider *Shenandoah,* which wrought havoc among whale ships in the Pacific in 1865, even though the Civil War was over. History is modified to permit the *Shenandoah* to refit in Hawaii, perhaps to advance a love affair of one of the ship's officers.

BROWN, MRS. ZENITH JONES ("Leslie Ford"). *Honolulu Story.* New York: Scribner, 1946. A "Colonel Primrose" story by a popular mystery writer, set in wartime Honolulu.

BURNS, EUGENE. *The Last King of Paradise.* New York: Pellegrini & Cudahy, 1952. A fictionized account by a journalist of the reign of Kalakaua, with imagined conversations and exploitation of the more shocking pagan customs.

CHIDSEY, DONALD BARR. *Lord of the Isles.* New York: Crown, 1954. A romance develops between a widow of one of the first company of missionaries and brawling Captain Johnny Lamb, trader and secret lover of Queen Kaahumanu, during three years of the early mission.

COFFMAN, VIRGINIA. *The House at Sandalwood.* New York: Arbor House, 1974. Just out of prison, Judith Cameron arrives at a small, imaginary Hawaiian island to look after her niece, wife of the master of the mansion of Sandalwood.

FRYE, PEARL. *The Narrow Bridge.* Boston: Little, Brown, 1947. In polished style, the story of the voyage of a girl from Honolulu to San Francisco during World War II includes sharply etched flashbacks to significant earlier scenes.

GILMAN, PETER. *Diamond Head.* New York: Coward-McCann, 1960. This novel draws heavily upon the local scene and presents the saga of a powerful island family. The author is a former Honolulu newspaper man.

HUIE, WILLIAM B. *The Revolt of Mamie Stover.* New York: Duell, Sloan & Pierce, 1951. Novel of a "madam" during World War II who enlarged her activities in the society of the period. A sequel is *Hotel Mamie Stover* (New York: C. N. Potter, 1963).

HUNTSBERRY, WILLIAM. *Harbor of the Little Boats.* New York: Rinehart, 1958. The small-boat harbor of Honolulu is the scene of a series of crimes that point the finger at Ring Bradford and keep Inspector Kealani busy. Professor Huntsberry is also author of another mystery novel, *Oscar Mooney's Head* (Rinehart, 1961).

KANE, HERBERT K. *Voyage.* Illus. Honolulu: Island Heritage, 1976. Recreation of a voyage from the South Pacific to Hawaii in pre-Cook times in a double-hulled vessel; includes paintings by the author.

KNIGHT, CLIFFORD. *The Affair of the Ginger Lei.* New York: Dodd, Mead, 1938. An apparently natural death on a yacht racing from California to Hawaii is revealed as a complicated murder. An abundance of clues, false and genuine, give the reader a chance to outguess the Honolulu police.

LONG, MAX. *Murder Between Dark and Dark.* New York: Lippincott, 1939. Komako Koa, a big Hawaiian policeman on a remote island coast, is called upon to solve a series of murders in the haole community. Koa is also called in after a group is isolated when boiling lava runs on both sides of a beach cottage in *The Lava Flow Murders*

(Lippincott, 1940). He is likewise the detective in *Death Goes Native* (Lippincott, 1941), when his friend Hastings Hoyt is threatened in a valley where a colony of haoles have retreated from the world.

LORING, EMILY. *Bright Skies.* Boston: Little, Brown, 1946. The suspenseful story of a Red Cross girl who is plunged into love and intrigue in World War II.

MACKAY, MARGARET M. *For All Men Born.* New York: John Day, 1943. A novel of Hawaii during the doomful, last months of 1941. *Homeward the Heart* (Day, 1944) is also a novel of World War II. *Sharon* (Day, 1948) is a historical novel of the 1880s in the islands.

MCKEE, RUTH ELEANOR. *The Lord's Anointed.* Garden City, N.Y.: Doubleday, 1934. Miss McKee, who came to Hawaii in 1926, adds an imaginary couple to the "First Company" of missionaries arriving in 1820. Constancy Williams bears eight children, is widowed, and lives beyond the century mark, into the period of American annexation. A sequel, *After a Hundred Years,* concerns Constancy's great-grandson, Hal Carrington, who returns to the islands in 1920 to take part in the centennial celebration of her arrival. Along with his bitterly cynical wife, Madge, Hal works out his destiny on a sugar plantation.

MIYAMOTO, KAZUE. *Hawaii: End of the Rainbow.* Rutland, Vt.: Tuttle, (paperback) 1964. A lengthy chronicle, in the form of a novel, of the Miyamoto family from the pioneering settlement days through internment during World War II and its aftermath. Dr. Miyamoto's story reveals courage, unhappiness, and reconciliation with life in American Hawaii.

MURAYAMA, MILTON. *All I Asking For is My Body.* San Francisco: Supa Press, 1975. A semi-autobiographical novel of the life of a Nisei schoolboy in a poor family living on Maui before World War II. Murayama served in the United States Army as an interpreter in India and China. He earned a bachelor's degree at the University of Hawaii and an M.A. at Columbia University. Warren Iwasa wrote of the book, in the *Hawaii Observer:* "While the two short pieces and the novel are not entirely successful as fiction, owing to their unshapeliness and their stylistic awkwardness (especially in translating what is supposed to be colloquial Japanese into English), they are important to have."

PATTON, BEATRICE AYER. *The Blood of the Shark.* Honolulu: Paradise of the Pacific, 1936, 1946. A sailor with Vancouver weds a chief's daughter during the reign of Kamehameha I. The author was wife of the fighting general of World War II.

SCHENCK, EARL. *Weeds of Violence.* Garden City, N.Y.: Doubleday, 1949. Jonathan Waincliff deserts his whale ship and escapes to an island where he falls in love with the native princess Healani. When the sweetheart of his youth arrives with a band of missionaries, he must make the decision of his life. Schenck is also author of two books about the South Seas, *Come Unto These Yellow Sands* (Indianapolis, Ind.: Bobbs-Merrill, 1940), an account of his wanderings in the South Pacific, and *Lean With the Wind* (New York: Whittlesey House, 1945; London: T. Werner Laurie, 1945), a novel set in Tahiti.

SHERIDAN, JUANITA. *The Kahuna Killer.* New York: Macmillan, 1951. Lily Wu solves the local murders in her own way. Two other detective stories about Lily are *The Mamo Murders* (1952) and *The Waikiki Widow* (1953; both published by Macmillan).

SHIROTA, JON HIROSHI. *Lucky Come Hawaii.* New York: Bantam, (paperback) 1965. The story of a Maui family during the year of the Pearl Harbor attack, by a Japanese-American. A second novel is *Pineapple White* (Los Angeles: Ohara, 1972), about an elderly Japanese gardener and his son, who wishes to marry a mainland haole girl.

THOMES, WILLIAM HENRY. *A Whaleman's Adventures in the Sandwich Islands and California.* Illus. Boston: Lea & Shepard, 1872. An amusing nineteenth-century tale of adventure.

WEBB, JEAN FRANCIS. *Somewhere Within This House.* New York: McKay, 1973. Ellen Sedgwick becomes governess to the blind little daughter of an aristocratic Waikiki family during the anti-royalist revolution of 1887. Mr. Webb is also author of *The Bride of Cairngore* (McKay, 1974), about Jessica Warren, who comes to Hawaii to transform a gloomy old mansion in the mountains into a luxury hotel and encounters a spooky legend.

WIDDEMER, MARGARET. *Lani.* Garden City, N.Y.: Doubleday, 1948. The period is 1889–90, when the "missionary set" came into conflict with the "court set" centering around headstrong King Kalakaua. Lani, a mission daughter, falls in love with Sir Mark Brent, but must leave for the far New Hebrides with her parents. On the ship she meets and marries an English trader. Then suddenly Mark reappears.

YATES, MARGARET. *Murder by the Yard.* New York: Macmillan, 1942. Davvy McLean, nurse wife of a Navy doctor, becomes suspicious of an advertisement in a Honolulu newspaper on December 4, 1941, that is presumably a code signal to the Japanese in Hawaii. Davvy also appears in an earlier detective story, *Midway to Murder* (Macmillan, 1941), set on pre-war Midway Island.

C. REFERENCE

All About Hawaii. Illus. Honolulu: Star-Bulletin, 1975. Founded in 1875 by Thomas G. Thrum as *Hawaiian Almanac and Annual,* this useful collection of facts has appeared under various titles for a century.

Atlas of Hawaii, compiled by the Department of Geography, University of Hawaii. Illus. Honolulu: University Press of Hawaii, 1973. An invaluable collection of maps, a gazetteer, and articles on natural environment, people and culture, the economy, and a bibliography.

Bernice Pauahi Bishop Museum, Honolulu. *Memoirs* and other publications.

BRYAN, EDWIN H., JR. *American Polynesia and the Hawaiian Chain.* rev. ed., Honolulu: Tongg, 1942. Much information, still valid, on the islands of the archipelago.

BUCK, PETER H. ("TE RANGI HIROA") *Arts and Crafts of Hawaii.* Illus. Bishop Museum Special Publication No. 45, 1957. (Reprinted in fourteen separate parts, 1974). Dr. Buck, former head of the Bernice P. Bishop Museum and a part-Maori, prepared this study of the material culture of ancient Hawaii. Chapters include details on animals, plants, implements of field and kitchen, houses, mats, baskets, clothing, canoes, fishing equipment, weapons, games, and religious objects. Buck is also author of *Vikings of the Sunrise* (New York: Stokes, 1938), a popularly written account of Polynesian migrations in the Pacific.

Carr, Elizabeth B. *Da Kine Talk: From Pidgin to Standard English in Hawaii.* Honolulu: University Press of Hawaii, 1972. Five stages in speech development by immigrant groups toward standard conversational English are analyzed. A glossary of Hawaiian pidgin terms is included. Carr has also published poetry.

Cox, J. Halley and Stasack, Edward. *Hawaiian Petroglyphs.* Honolulu: Bishop Museum Press, 1970. A complete listing of sites of rock drawings and a general description of the making of these carved records, which often have a unique artistic charm.

Current Hawaiiana: Quarterly Bibliography of Publications on Hawaii. Sinclair Library, University of Hawaii, 1944—. A mimeographed, comprehensive listing sent free to libraries and other institutions.

Dictionary Catalog of the Hawaiian Collection, University of Hawaii. Boston: G. K. Hall, 1963. 4 vol. A photographic reproduction of catalog cards in the largest collection of Hawaii and Pacific materials in the state. Since publication, the catalog numbers have been shifted from the Dewey to the Library of Congress system.

Fairfax, Geoffrey W. *The Architecture of Honolulu.* Illus. Honolulu: Island Heritage, 1972. A record of existing buildings that reflect the eclectic styles to be found in the city.

Finney, Ben R. and Houston, James D. *Surfing: The Sport of Hawaiian Kings.* Rutland, Vt.: Tuttle, 1966. A history of surfing from ancient times to the present, by a University of Hawaii professor.

Handy, E. S. C. *et al. Ancient Hawaiian Civilization.* Honolulu: Kamehameha Schools Press, 1933; rev. ed., Rutland, Vt.: Tuttle, 1965. A series of some thirty school lectures by such authorities on pre-Cook life as Sir Peter H. Buck, Kenneth P. Emory, E. H. Bryan, Jr., and Henry P. Judd.

Hawaiian Historical Society, Publications. An *Index* (Honolulu: Hawaiian Historical Society, 1968), compiled by Charles R. Hunter, analyzes papers and annual reports by subject; there are separate lists of illustrations, maps, diagrams, and tables, as well as a glossary of Hawaiian words.

Hawaiian Journal of History. Honolulu: Hawaiian Historical Society, 1967—. An annual collection of scholarly articles. See also *Hawaiian Historical Review: Selected Readings,* ed. Richard A. Greer (Honolulu: Hawaiian Historical Society,1969).

Horwitz, Robert H. and Meller, Norman. *Land and Politics in Hawaii.* Honolulu: University of Hawaii Press, 1966. An account of various attempts to legislate land reforms.

Hosaka, Edward Y. *Sport Fishing in Hawaii.* Honolulu: Bond, 1944. A practical handbook on shoreline fishing, with many handy hints.

Index to the Honolulu Advertiser and Honolulu Star-Bulletin, 1929—. A subject index of articles in the two leading newspapers of Honolulu appears in several volumes; the most recent is 1974.

JACKSON, FRANCES; CONRAD, AGNES; and BANNICK, NANCY. *Old Honolulu: A Guide to Oahu's Historic Buildings.* Honolulu: Historic Buildings Task Force, 1969. Eighty-seven buildings of importance are featured.

JUDD, BERNICE. *Voyages to Hawaii Before 1860.* Honolulu: Hawaiian Mission Children's Society, 1929; rev. ed. (with Helen Y. Lind), Honolulu: University Press of Hawaii, 1973. Factual guide to ship visits, with chronological list of voyages, index of vessels and persons, and bibliography.

LEIB, AMOS P. *Hawaiian Legends in English: An Annotated Bibliography.* Honolulu: University of Hawaii Press, 1949. An invaluable key to the study of Hawaiian legends and lore. The bibliography, complete through the 1940s, is supplemented by comments on sources, style, and content of the individual items. The author also gives a brief critical history of the translation of Hawaiian myths and legends and discusses in some detail the backgrounds and methods of the more important translators, from the early voyagers to modern retellers such as Padraic Colum. A supplement to this valuable work is in preparation. Dr. Leib is also author of *The Many Islands of Polynesia* (New York: Scribner, 1972), a volume that presents many aspects of Hawaii.

Men of Hawaii: A Biographical Reference Library . . . Illus. Honolulu: Star-Bulletin, 1917. A who's who of island notables, revised at intervals of several years. In 1954 the title was changed to *Men and Women of Hawaii.* The most recent volume is dated 1972. Of special interest is *Builders of Hawaii,* which incorporates *Men of Modern Hawaii,* 1925.

Missionary Album. Honolulu: Hawaiian Mission Children's Society, 1901, 1937, 1969. Portraits and biographies of the missionaries sent by the American Board of Commissioners of Foreign Missions. The 1901 title was *Portraits of American Protestant Missionaries to Hawaii.*

MURDOCH, CLARE G. and GOTANDA, MASAE. *Basic Hawaiiana.* Honolulu: State of Hawaii, Dept. of Education, 1969. A selected, annotated bibliography covering books in all areas of writing, from mythology to cookery.

PATTERSON, O. B. *Surf-Riding, Its Thrill and Techniques.* Rutland, Vt.: Tuttle, 1960. History and legends are included in this account of modern surfing.

PUKUI, MARY K. and ELBERT, SAMUEL H. *Hawaiian Dictionary.* Honolulu: University Press of Hawaii, 1971. Combines the earlier Hawaiian-English and English-Hawaiian dictionaries, with new supplements. The standard work on the Hawaiian language, by a part-Hawaiian scholar and a professor emeritus of Oceanic languages, University of Hawaii (see No. 12).

ROBERTS, HELEN HEFFRON. *Ancient Hawaiian Music.* New York: Dover, 1967. A scholarly treatise on the subject, covering instruments, chants, dances, and localities where music was to be found. A reprint of Bishop Museum Bulletin No. 29, 1926.

SCHMITT, ROBERT C. *Demographic Statistics of Hawaii, 1778–1965.*

Honolulu: University of Hawaii Press, 1968. A comprehensive documentation and evaluation of sources by the State Statistican, providing vital statistics during the post-Cook era. The book is more than a collection of figures; it demonstrates various major and minor themes in island history.

SCOTT, EDWARD B. *The Saga of the Sandwich Islands.* Illus. Lake Tahoe, Nev.: Sierra-Tahoe Publishing Co., 1968. A voluminous collection of photographs dealing with the island of Oahu, with lengthy captions and an index.

Index of Authors and Editors

Production Notes

The text of this book has been designed by Roger J. Eggers and typeset on the Unified Composing System by the design & production staff of The University Press of Hawaii.

The text and display typeface is English Times.

Offset presswork and binding is the work of Vail-Ballou Press. Text paper is Glatfelter P & S Offset, basis 55.